KEY FACTS

EMPLOYMENT
LAW

SECOND EDITION

CHRIS TURNER

Hodder Arnold

Orders: please contact Bookpoint Ltd, 130 Milton Park, Abingdon, Oxon OX14 4SB. Telephone: (44) 01235 827720. Fax: (44) 01235 400454. Lines are open from 9.00 - 5.00, Monday to Saturday, with a 24 hour message answering service. You can also order through our website www.hoddereducation.co.uk.

British Library Cataloguing in Publication Data
A catalogue record for this title is available from The British Library.

ISBN-13: 978 0 340 88947 3

First Edition published 2002
Second Edition published 2005
Impression number   10 9 8 7 6 5 4
Year   2008 2007

Cover design by Stewart Larking
Typeset by Transet Limited, Coventry, England.
Printed in Great Britain for Hodder Arnold, an imprint of Hodder Education, a member of the Hodder Headline Group, 338 Euston Road, London NW1 3BH by Cox & Wyman Ltd, Reading, Berks.

CONTENTS

Preface   vii

Chapter 1 The historical background to employment law   **1**
1.1 The development of employment protections   1
1.2 The importance of EU membership to employment law   4

Chapter 2 Employment status   **7**
2.1 Distinguishing employment and self-employment   7
2.2 Tests of employment status   10

Chapter 3 Contract of employment   **13**
3.1 Formation of employment contracts   14
3.2 The section 1 statement   16
3.3 The incorporation of express terms   18
3.4 Collective agreements   20
3.5 Works rules   23
3.6 Restraint of trade clauses   25
3.7 Garden leave clauses   29
3.8 Grievance procedure   31
3.9 Disciplinary procedures   33

Chapter 4 Implied terms   **39**
4.1 The process of implying terms   40
4.2 The implied duties of employers   41
4.3 The implied duties of employees   42

Chapter 5 Statutory protections   **45**
5.1 Maternity   46
5.2 Parental leave, dependant care leave, adoption leave   50
5.3 Wages   51
5.4 Guarantee payments   57

Chapter 6 Discrimination   **58**
6.1 Equal pay   59
6.2 Sex discrimination   63
6.3 Race discrimination   71
6.4 Disability discrimination   75
6.5 Discrimination on trade union grounds   78
6.6 Discrimination and religion and belief   83
6.7 Pursuing discrimination claims   84

Chapter 7 Health and safety law   **87**
7.1 Common law provisions   88
7.2 Statutory and EU protections   92

Chapter 8 TUPE transfers   **99**
8.1 General background   99
8.2 To whom regulations apply   100
8.3 The nature of a transfer for TUPE purposes   101
8.4 The effect of the transfer   103
8.5 Dismissal on transfer   104
8.6 Consultations   106

Chapter 9 Termination of employment   **107**
9.1 Continuity, notice and dismissal   108
9.2 Wrongful dismissal   111
9.3 Unfair dismissal   113
9.4 Redundancy   125

Chapter 10 Institutions and procedure   **132**
10.1 Courts and tribunals hearing employment cases   132
10.2 Tribunal procedure   134

Index   **140**

PREFACE

The Key Facts series is designed to give a clear view of each subject. This will be useful to students when tackling new topics and is invaluable as a revision aid. Most chapters open with an outline in diagram form of the points covered in that chapter. The points are then developed in list form to make learning easier. Supporting cases are given throughout by name and for some complex areas the facts of cases are given throughout to reinforce the point being made.

The topics covered for Employment Law include all of the main areas of all mainstream syllabuses. Employment Law is an exciting and rapidly changing and expanding area, and a very practical and useful subject.

The law is stated as I believe it to be at 1st January 2005.

CHAPTER 1

THE HISTORICAL BACKGROUND TO EMPLOYMENT LAW

1.1 THE DEVELOPMENT OF EMPLOYMENT PROTECTIONS

1.1.1 The history and background to employment law

1. Regulating employment goes back as far as Statute of Labourers 1399 and Statute of Artificers and Apprentices 1652.
2. So while employment is based on a contractual relationship it has always been subject to statutory intervention.
3. Modern employment law begins with the so-called 'master and servant laws' of the nineteenth century and always an unequal relationship (*Latter v Braddell* (1881)).

1.1.2 The scope of employment law

1. Divides into three neat areas:
   (i)   industrial safety law;
   (ii) employment law;
   (iii) industrial relations law.
2. Industrial safety law developed through nineteenth century statutes, common law duty, the Health & Safety at Work Act 1974 and EC intervention.
3. Employment law is based on contract law.
4. Industrial relations have always been led by politics, and subject to violent change and great controversy.

1.1.3 Development of employment rights and protections

1. Early twentieth century saw other measures to curb exploitation e.g. Wages Councils.

2. In the 1950s, conditions were generally settled by free collective bargaining – 'collective *laissez faire*' Otto Kahn-Freund.

3. Move towards a basic 'floor of rights' emerged in the 1960s:

- Contracts of Employment Act 1963;
- Redundancy Payments Act 1965;
- Trade Disputes Act 1965 reversed (*Rookes v Barnard* (1964)).

4. Donovan Commission 1968 suggested pay bargaining at local level to improve productivity and resolve differences quickly.

5. Labour followed this with White Paper 'In place of strife'.

6. Industrial Relations Act 1971 tried to create framework for industrial relations, failed but introduced unfair dismissal.

7. Labour 1974–1979 introduced consolidation package with:

- Employment Protection Act 1975, Employment Protection Consolidation Act 1978 – on employment rights;
- Sex Discrimination Act 1975, Race Relations Act 1976.

8. EC has also been major source of increased employee rights:

- though effect much reduced by hostility of Conservative governments 'socialism entering by back door';
- certain law forced on government during period often in infringement proceedings in European Court of Justice e.g. Equal Pay Directive 75/117 in Equal Pay (Amendment) Regulations 1983; Acquired Rights Directive 77/187 in Transfer of Undertakings (Protection of Employment) Regulations 1981;
- and EC case law had similar effect (*Marshall v Southampton and SW Havant A H A* (1986)).

1.1.4 Reductions of employee rights

1. Legislation of 1980s–1990s restricted rights and protections:

- right to return after pregnancy: Employment Act 1980;
- unfair dismissal qualifying period increased;
- deposits required for Employment Tribunals by Employment Act 1989;
- rights to particulars of disciplinary procedures for small firms (less than 20 employees) in Employment Act 1989;

- Wages Councils abolished in Trade Union Reform and Employment Rights Act 1993;
- criminal sanctions for unauthorised deductions from pay, abolished in the Wages Act 1986;
- restrictions on heavy work and night work in factories for women removed in the Employment Act 1989;
- time off for trade union activities restricted;
- trade union immunities curtailed by Employment Act 1980, and 1982, and Trade Union Act 1984;
- government of 1980s and 1990s resisted employment protection measures required under EC law;
- although mass of legislation built up led to introduction of consolidating Act – Employment Rights Act 1996.

1.1.5 Advancement of employee rights

1. Current government is committed to employee protection.
2. Signed Social Chapter so EU could introduce social legislation.
3. A number of measures have been introduced:

- Working Time Regulations 1998 – introduced minimum conditions for working time, rest periods, holidays, night work etc. from Working Time Directive;
- National Minimum Wage Act 1998 – reintroduced minimum wage rates;
- Public Interest Disclosure Act 1998 – for whistle blowing;
- Data Protection Act 1998 – regulation on protected data;
- Unfair Dismissal Order 1999 – qualifying period to one year;
- Employment Relations Act 1999 – including rules on union recognition, representation on disciplinary and grievance procedures, and family-friendly policies such as parental leave, dependant relative leave.
- Implementation of EC Part Time Workers Directive, Fixed Term Contract Directive, and Works Councils Directive, Burden of Proof Directive 97/80, Equal Treatment in Employment and Occupation Directive 2000/78, Equal Treatment Between Persons Irrespective of Racial or Ethnic Origin Directive 2000/43.

4. The Human Rights Act 1998 also has an impact on the employment relationship.

1.2 THE IMPORTANCE OF EU MEMBERSHIP TO EMPLOYMENT LAW

1.2.1 Issues concerning membership

1. UK a member by (i) signing treaties; (ii) EC Act 1972.
2. S2(1) incorporated all existing EU law, and all future EU law.
3. 'Direct applicability' appropriate to much EU law, and s2(2) gives power to implement EU law by delegated legislation.
4. Single European Act 1986 signed by all members (led to EC (Amendment) Act 1986) new voting system in Council, and new A138 (ex A118a) inserted in treaty on HASAW.
5. Treaty of European Union 1992 (Maastricht):

- created Union, and concept of citizenship;
- 'social chapter' agreed by all member states (originally UK had an opt out created in the Protocol);
- 'subsidiarity' – if possible to deal with at state level, no EU action unless treaty objective thwarted (UK demand).

6. Treaty of Amsterdam 1997 – UK signed up to Social Chapter.

1.2.2 Relevance to UK labour law

1. A137 (ex A118) requires harmonised laws on 'employment, labour law and working conditions, basic and advanced training, social security, protection against occupational accidents and diseases, occupational hygiene, trade unions and collective bargaining' – but any legislation requires unanimous vote.
2. A39 (ex A48) grants free movement of workers, so combined effect should be fully integrated system.
3. Treaty requires maintaining existing standards in member states, so harmonisation should upgrade not downgrade.
4. Period up to 1979 very active for developments in labour law:

- equal pay directive 75/117;

- equal access directive 76/207;
- non-discriminatory social security benefits 79/7;
- collective dismissals directive 75/129;
- acquired rights directive 77/187.

5. But from then until 1997 stagnation through UK veto.
6. Many infringement actions against UK and cases involving interpretation of EU law (*MacCarthy's v Smith* (1979)).
7. Constant tension between Conservative government of the 1980s and EU, government wanted deregulation and standards determined by market, EU wanted minimum floor of worker rights.
8. Led to Community Charter of Fundamental Social Rights of Workers 1989 – signed by all except UK.
9. Basis of 'Social Chapter' at Maastricht – agreed by all except UK – (created in Protocol with UK opt out).
10. By A239 a Protocol was annexed to treaty on which previous government tried unsuccessfully to rely e.g. to resist Working Time Directive 93/104 – altered with change of government.

1.2.3 The Supranational Legal Order

1. EU law is found in:
- treaty articles, substantive e.g. A141 (ex A119), or procedural e.g. A249 (ex A189);
- legislation (regulations, directives and decisions – but in labour law mainly directives);
- ECJ case law and general principles e.g. proportionality.

2. First key principles for law to work is supremacy: EU law is superior to national law (*Costa v ENEL* (1964)).

- National courts must disapply inconsistent domestic law (*R v Sec of State for Transport ex parte Factortame* (1990)).
- National court may strike down national legislation even though the body has no directly effective rights. (*R v Secretary of State for Employment ex parte EOC* (1994)).

3. Second key principle is direct effect: means if right granted by EU law citizen can enforce it in national courts:

- straightforward with legally complete provisions substantive treaty articles A141 and (*Defrenne v Sabena* (1976));
- but not with Directives.

1.2.4 Direct effect and directives

1. Defined in A249 (ex A189) as 'binding as to the result to be achieved' – so left to member state to implement.
2. Not horizontally directly effective – no right as between citizen and citizen (*Duke v GEC Reliance* (1988)).
3. But vertically directly effective (*Marshall v Southampton AHA* (1986)).
4. ECJ do not like idea that citizen can be denied rights so have developed other means to protect rights:
   - indirect effect – 'Von Colson principle' – from A10 must construe national law to give effect to directive;
   - and can give rise to an action for damages against the state (*Francovitch v Italian Republic* (1992)).

1.2.5 UK implementation of EU law

1. Can be by Act (Social Security Act 1986 implementing Directive 86/378 on occupational social security schemes) or:
   - by statutory instrument (Equal Pay (Amendment) Regulations 1983 implementing Directive 75/117), or
   - by UK courts accepting principles of vertical direct effect, or
   - following infringement proceedings under A226 (ex A169) e.g. Commission v UK 61/81 and Equal Pay (Amendment) Regulations 1983 and *Hayward v Camel Laird*, or
   - following A234 (ex A177) references e.g. failure to properly implement Directive 76/207 led to decision in *Marshall v Southampton & South West Havant HA* (1986) and Sex Discrimination Act 1986, or
   - the UK courts applying EU principles e.g. Employment Protection (Part-time Employees) Regulations followed (*R v Secretary of State for Employment ex parte EOC* (1994)).

CHAPTER 2

EMPLOYMENT STATUS

2.1 DISTINGUISHING EMPLOYMENT AND SELF-EMPLOYMENT

2.1.1 The employment relationship

1. By s230 Employment Rights Act 1996 an employee is '… an individual who has entered into or works under a contract of employment …'.
2. Employer might be sole trader, partnership, company, unincorporated association, private individual.
3. Employer's needs vary enormously on hiring 'labour' – may want permanent staff; temporary, part time or casual; or highly skilled for specific tasks.
4. Common characteristics e.g. selection, some form of supervision, payment of a wage or salary – statutory definition is inadequate – so traditional tests are used.
5. Traditional distinction is between:
   - a contract *of* service (employee); and
   - a contract *for* services (independent contractors).
6. Distinction important because of character of work: 62.3% of households budget from wages, but 10% now from self-employment, a fourfold increase from the 1970s.
7. There are three key factors in defining employment:
   - the reasons for distinguishing;
   - tests which determine which classification applies;
   - types of work relationships that defy easy description.

2.1.2 The purpose of distinguishing

1. Independent contractors may be better off financially but can be disadvantaged if injured – so there are advantages and disadvantages in both classifications.

2. The differences are determined by the consequences of whatever classification.

	EMPLOYEES	SELF-EMPLOYED
Common law terms	A contract of employment includes many implied common law terms.	A contract for services is usually only subject to its express terms.
Statutory employment rights	Employees enjoy many protections e.g. redundancy, maternity etc. (see Employment Rights Act 1996).	Most protections are denied to self-employed.
Discrimination	Employees are covered by discrimination law.	Self-employed are also covered by discrimination law.
Health and safety	High level of care owed to employees – in statute (HASAW 74), and in common law.	Lower duty and virtually no common law duty – because independent contractors have the expertise to guard their own safety.
Breach of a statutory duty	Some statutes, particularly in industrial safety, may provide a civil action for breach of a duty, as well as commonly imposing criminal sanctions e.g. fencing machinery.	Such duties are rarely applicable to independent contractors. If there is a non-delegable duty to ensure equipment is used as well as provided it will be owed to both employees and self-employed.
Vicarious liability	Employers are commonly liable for the torts of their employees committed in the course of their employment.	Such liability will rarely operate in respect of hired independent contractors – unless the hirer directed the contractor to do the tort.
Taxation	Schedule E. PAYE. Deducted at source on each pay period.	Schedule D. Annual payment following submission of accounts. Advantage of setting off expenses. But self-employed may be liable to register for VAT.
Welfare benefits	Class 1 NI contributions deducted from wages. Employees may claim all available benefits.	Class 2 or Class 4 contributions made by the self-employed person. Minimal benefits available.
Insolvency/ bankruptcy	Employees are preferential creditors and can recover money owed from the liquidator as well as applying for redundancy payments from the Secretary of State.	Self-employed are not. As well as losing the money they may be owed – they may in turn be forced out of business as a result.
Benefits to the employer	Greater degree of control over the work. Possibility of greater diversification among the workforce. Possibly greater disciplinary powers. Collective bargaining more available.	Reduced expenditure on administration. No levy for industrial training. Trade unions are less likely to recruit among the self-employed.

Consequences of distinguishing between employees and self-employed

Tests of employment

Control test:
- from servant is due obedience and respect, from master protection and good treatment (*Limland v Stephens*);
- useful for loaned employees (*Mersey Docks & Harbour Board v Coggins & Griffiths*).

Organisation or integration test:
- because of inadequacy of control test (*Cassidy v Minister of Health*);
- depends on whether person part and parcel of business (*Stevenson, Jordan & Harrison v MacDonald & Evans*);
- useful for highly skilled (*Whittaker v Minister of Pensions*).

Economic reality or multiple test:
- From *Ready Mixed Concrete v Minister of Pensions* 3-part test:
- agreement to supply skill in return for wages;
- express or implied submission to employer's control;
- nothing in contract inconsistent with employment;
- can consider/weigh all factors e.g. ownership of tools, degree of independence, tax and NI liability, degree of financial risk etc.

Self description:
- test may be '… is person performing services in business on his own account …' (*Market Investigations v Minister of Social Services*);
- strong but inconclusive evidence (*Massey v Crown Life Insurance*);
- courts look more to substance of relationship than label applied (*Ferguson v John Dawson Ltd*).

TESTING EMPLOYMENT STATUS

Special forms of work relationship
- Labour only – usually self-employed (*Emerald Construction Co. v Lowthian*).
- Casual – usually self-employed (*Carmichael v National Power plc*).
- Agency staff – usually self-employed unless works for same client with enough control (*Motorola Ltd v Davidson*).
- Outworkers – usually self-employed (*Westhall Richardson v Roulson*) – but may gain employment protections (*Nethermere (St Neots) v Taverna*).
- Hospital staff – should usually be vicarious liability (*Cassidy v MOH*).
- Directors – can be employed (*Lee v Lee's Air Farming*).
- Office holders – can be either (*Barthorpe v Exeter Diocesan Board of Finance*).
- Crown employees – some may lose employment protection rights.
- Part-time workers – now have pro rata rights with full timers – Part-Time Workers (Prevention of Less Favourable Treatment) Regulations 2000.

2.2 TESTS OF EMPLOYMENT STATUS

2.2.1 The tests for measuring employee status

1. No adequate statutory definition so courts devised tests.

2. Because of diverse character of work no test is absolute.

3. Modern approach is to balance out all relevant factors.

4. The Control Test:

- oldest test – from master/servant rules, defined by Lord Kenyon in *Limland v Stephens* (1801) '... from the servant is due obedience and respect; from the master protection and good treatment ...' or;
- McArdie in *Performing Rights Society Ltd v Mitchell & Booker* (1924) '... nature and degree of detailed control ...';
- useful in straightforward employment but impractical if more sophisticated (*Collins v Herts CC* (1947));
- still a factor in multiple test;
- can determine vicarious liability in temporary transfers (*Mersey Docks & Harbour Board v Coggins & Griffith* (1947)) compare with *Garrard v Southey & Co. & Standard Cables Ltd* (1952).

5. The Organisation Test:

- developed because of defects of control test – Denning in *Cassidy v Minister of Health* (1951);
- '... is person part and parcel of organisation ...' (*Stevenson, Jordan & Harrison v MacDonald & Evans* (1952));
- so test can prove useful in respect of highly-skilled staff (*Whittaker v Minister of Pensions* (1967)).

6. The Ordinary Person Test:

- is there '... contract of service within meaning an ordinary person would give ...' (*Collins v Herts CC*).

7. The Indicia Test:

- devised by Lord Thankerton in *Short v Henderson* (1946) based on four indicators (indicia):
  - (i) master's power of selection;
  - (ii) presence of wage payment;
  - (iii) master's right to control;
  - (iv) right of suspension or dismissal.

- but points only to a contract.

8. The Multiple (or Economic Reality) Test:
- derives from judgement of MacKenna J in
  Ready Mixed Concrete Ltd v Minister of Pensions (1968);
- three part test – contract of employment exists if:
  (i) agree to provide work and skill for wages;
  (ii) express or implied submission to control;
  (iii) nothing significant inconsistent with employment.
- pragmatic approach – takes all factors into account, e.g.
  degree of control; obligation to give work; or do work;
  provision of tools, equipment; tax and NI payment;
  freedom to do other work; holiday entitlement, notice,
  expenses; financial risk; duration of engagement.
- tribunal weighs rather than counts factors (*Hitchcock v Post
  Office* (1980));
- so e.g. a power to delegate possible in employment contract
  (*MacFarlane v Glasgow City Council* (2001)).

9. Self Description:
- test may be as simple as '… is person performing services in
  business on his own account …?' (*Market Investigations v
  Minister of Social Services* (1969));
- or could be asked 'Are you your own boss?' (*Withers v
  Flackwell Heath Supporters Club* (1981));
- is strong but inconclusive evidence (*Massey v Crown Life
  Insurance* (1978);
- courts look more to substance of relationship than label
  applied (*Ferguson v John Dawson Ltd* (1976)).

2.2.2 Special forms of work relationship

1. Labour only sub-contractors (the lump):
- labourers in construction industry – self-employed
  (*Emerald Construction Co. Ltd v Lowthian* (1966));
- tax exemption certificate (715) shows self-employment.

2. Casual employment:
- usual test is mutuality of obligations (*O'Kelly & Others v
  Trust House Forte plc* (1983));

- and often seen as self-employed (*Carmichael v National Power plc* (1998)).

3. Agency staff – usually seen as self-employed – but can be employees if working consistently for same client who has sufficient control (*Motorola Ltd v Davidson* (2001)). An implied contractual relationship may be found (*Dacas v Brook Street Bureau* (2004)).

4. Outworkers:
   - historically seen as independent so have few rights;
   - originally tested under integration test (*Westhall Richardson v Roulson* (1954));
   - but now under economic reality test (*Airfix Footwear Ltd v Cope* (1978));
   - employment protection legislation has also helped (*Nethermere (St Neots) v Taverna* (1984)).

5. Hospital staff – Denning in *Cassidy v Minister of Health* (1951) felt there should always be vicarious liability.

6. Directors – may be employed or self-employed leading to strange results (*Lee v Lee's Air Farming Ltd* (1961)).

7. Office holders:
   - may not be employed so have privileges e.g. judges;
   - and e.g. a registrar can only be dismissed by the Registrar General not by the council (*Lincolnshire CC v Hopper* (2002));
   - but some are recognised as employees (*Barthorpe v Exeter Diocesan Board of Finance* (1979)).

8. Crown employees – not all employment protections apply.

9. Part-time employees:
   - until recently had fairly limited rights;
   - ECJ in *R v Secretary of State for Employment ex p EOC* (1994) held EU law not properly implemented, so equal rights extended in Employment Protection (Part-Time Employees) Regulations 1995;
   - Part-Time Workers (Prevention of Less Favourable Treatment) Regulations 2000 gives pro rata rights and applies to workers not just employees but only direct discrimination is covered.

CHAPTER 3

CONTRACT OF EMPLOYMENT

Form and writing
- Can be oral, written or by conduct.
- But requires evidence in s1 statement.
- Written contract needed for:
  - apprenticeship;
  - merchant seamen;
  - returning from maternity;
  - some fixed-term contracts.

Formalities
- Offer of work unconditionally accepted.
- Offer can be individual or to whole world (*Carlill v Carbolic Smoke Ball Co*) – and can be subject to condition precedent e.g. satisfactory reference.
- Intent to create legal relations (*R v Lord Chancellor's Dept ex parte Nangle*).
- Consideration i.e. work in return of a wage.

FORMATION

Illegality
- Unenforceable in tribunal because contrary to public policy (*Corby v Morrison*).
- Employee may lose statutory rights (*Cole v Stacey*).
- Illegal contract may later become legal (*Attridge v Jaydees Newsagents Ltd*).
- Not enforceable just because illegality performed (*Coral Leisure Group v Barnett*).
- Knowledge of illegality loses rights (*Tomlinson v Dick Evans 'u' Drive Ltd*).

Minority
- Bound by contract of service substantially for his benefit (*Clements v LNWR*).
- But not if substantially detrimental (*De Francesco v Barnum*).

3.1 FORMATION OF EMPLOYMENT CONTRACTS

3.1.1 The Form of the Contract of Employment

1. Inevitably covered by basic rules of contract law.
2. Can be formal, informal, oral or in writing.
3. Can arise from complex negotiations or from conduct.
4. Or contract may be implied by parties dealing with each other over time (*Dacas v Brook Street Bureau* (2004)).

3.1.2 The Contract and the requirement of writing

1. No general requirement for contract to be in writing (but does require written evidence of the s1 statement).
2. Exceptions where writing is required include:
   - an employee operating under a fixed-term contract may elect in writing to exclude redundancy rights;
   - contracts of apprenticeship must be signed as well as in writing;
   - the Merchant Shipping Act requires seamen's contracts to be in writing and signed by both employee and employer;
   - there are complex rules regarding maternity (and more new rules to come), generally however, an employer may request in writing and an employee may then be obliged to reply in writing stating her intention to return to work.

3.1.3 Contractual formalities

1. There must be an offer of work which is unconditionally accepted (but it could be an offer to work).
2. The offer may be oral or made through an advertisement (in which case it can obviously be made to the whole world (*Carlill v Carbolic Smokeball Co.* (1893)).
3. An offer of employment can be made subject to a condition precedent e.g. a satisfactory reference or medical examination (*Wishart v National Association of CAB'x Ltd* (1990)).

4. Acceptance may be in any form e.g. a handshake.
5. The parties must intend to create legal relations (*R v Lord Chancellor's Department ex p Nangle* (1992)).
6. There must be consideration for the agreement (which would be executory – the promise of work for wages).

3.1.4 Minority and the contract of employment

1. This is as for minors' contracts generally.
2. A minor (a person under 18) is bound by a contract for employment, training or education that is substantially for his/her benefit (*Clements v London & North Western Railway Co.* (1894) and (*Chaplin v Leslie Frewin (Publishers) Ltd* (1966)).
3. If the contract is against the minor's best interests it will not bind him/her (*De Francesco v Barnum* (1890)).

3.1.5 Illegal contracts and employment

1. An illegal contract cannot be enforced in the tribunal.
2. Such contracts may be contrary to public policy at common law or prohibited by statute, in either case the contract may prove to be unenforceable by either party (*Corby v Morrison* (1980)).
3. The employee may lose statutory rights as a result (*Cole v Stacey* (1974)).
4. Though an illegal contract may later become legal (*Attridge v Jaydees Newsagents Ltd* (unreported 1980 EAT)).
5. A legally formed contract illegally performed is not automatically unenforceable (*Coral Leisure Group Ltd v Barnett* (1981)).
6. It is usually the employee's knowledge of the illegality which leads to a loss of rights under it (*Tomlinson v Dick Evans 'U' Drive Ltd* (1978)).

3.2 THE SECTION 1 STATEMENT

3.2.1 The Legal Status of the s1 Statement

1. Not the contract (*Robertson v British Gas Corp* (1983)).
2. But evidence of the contractual terms – which is strong if sole evidence (*Gascol Conversions Ltd v Mercer* (1974)).

3.2.2 Enforcement

1. If no statement is provided or necessary details are omitted then employee can make reference to tribunal.
2. Tribunal may confirm, amend, but not rewrite it.
3. And can declare terms parties meant to include, but not interpret them (*Cuthbertson v AML Distributors* (1975)).

WRITTEN PARTICULARS REQUIRED IN THE S1 STATEMENT
Employment Rights Act 1996 s1 – within eight weeks of employment, employer must provide employee with written statement containing following:

Basic information	a) names of both employer and employee; b) date of commencement of employment; c) date of commencement of continuous employment.
Information to be given at specified date not more than seven days before statement is given	a) scale of remuneration, method of calculating pay, pay period; b) terms concerning hours of work; c) holiday entitlements (including public holidays and holiday pay); provisions for sickness & sick pay; pension rights & schemes; d) periods of notice on both sides; e) job title; f) period of employment if not permanent; g) place(s) of work; h) details of collective agreements affecting conditions; i) specific details for overseas working.
Other key factors	(1) If no particulars are to be entered under any of these heads then that fact should be stated. (2) The statement may refer the employee to other documents which give more detailed explanations, but only where the employee will have adequate access to these during his/her employment. (3) The statement must be given even though the employment is terminated within the two months.
Additional information	a) details of disciplinary rules; and since Employment Act 2002 details of disciplinary procedures; b) details of grievance procedure. **N.B. changes to matters specified in the statement should be made known to employee within one month of the change.**

Range and character of express terms
- Parties can agree any terms that are legal.
- So can be unequal relationship.
- S1 ERA requires written statement on minimum range of terms.
- Express terms can include:
  - i) specific terms agreed by parties;
  - ii) everything required to be in s1 statement;
  - iii) things referred to but contained in other documents.

Range and character of express terms
- Terms can be implied also.
- Better to have express terms in writing (*Stubbs v Trower, Still & Keeling*).
- Written statement should accurately reflect actual agreement (*Nelson v BBC*).
- Express oral terms may override written statement (*Hawker Siddeley Power Engineering Ltd v Rump*).
- Either party can accept breaches by the other party or count them as grounds for dismissal/constructive dismissal.
- Based on test of fairness (*Martin v Solus Schall*).

INCORPORATING EXPRESS TERMS

Interpreting express terms
- Court decides if term consistent with employment (*Cole v Midland Display Ltd*).
- But cannot change job description (*Redbridge LBC v Flashman*).
- Can use job advert to aid construction (*Tayside Regional Council v McIntosh*).
- Traditional view – employee bound by any term agreed to (*Rank Xerox v Churchill*).
- Modern view – express terms should be exercised reasonably (*United Bank Ltd v Akhtar*).
- Unilateral variation of terms is impossible (*Hayes v Securities and Facilities Division*).
- *Contra preferentum* rule applies (*Skilton v T & K Home Improvements Ltd*).

Advantages and disadvantages
Advantages:
- less room for dispute;
- saves time and money;
- can be broadly stated giving employer greater scope for flexible working.

Disadvantages:
- may be drafted too narrowly for employer's needs;
- may be construed narrowly by tribunal.

3.3 THE INCORPORATION OF EXPRESS TERMS

3.3.1 The range and character of express terms

1. Parties may agree on any terms – subject to general principles of law.
2. So may reflect inadequate balance – but not slavery (Somersett's case).
3. Negotiations may mention pay, holidays, hours, etc. – s1 ERA 1996 requires written notice of certain terms, so there is a lower limit to create certainty.
4. Express terms can be oral or written, and may include:
   - specific terms agreed by parties;
   - everything required to be in the s1 statement;
   - terms contained in other documents specifically referred to in the s1 statement.

3.3.2 The significance of the express terms

1. Not all terms are expressed, many are implied either by custom or statute.
2. It is preferable for express terms to be in writing (*Stubbs v Trower, Still & Keeling* (1987)).
3. So written statement needs to accurately represent actual agreement (*Nelson v BBC* (1977)).
4. Express oral terms can override the statement (*Hawker Siddeley Power Engineering Ltd v Rump* (1979)).
5. Either party can accept breaches by the other party or count them as grounds for dismissal if by employee, or for a claim for constructive dismissal if by employer.
6. In either case established tests of fairness/unfairness will be used (*Martin v Solus Schall* (1979)).

3.3.3 Interpreting express terms

1. Courts decide if term is consistent with an employment relationship (*Cole v Midland Display Ltd* (1973)).
2. But interpretation cannot be used in effect to change the job description (*Redbridge LBC v Fishman* (1978)).
3. Extrinsic material e.g. job advertisements may be used to ascertain the meaning of terms (*Tayside Regional Council v McIntosh* (1982)).
4. But not to override express terms (*Deeley v BREL* (1980)).
5. Traditionally felt if employee agrees a term then is bound by it however harsh (*Rank Xerox Ltd v Churchill* (1988)).
6. More modern view is that express terms should be exercised reasonably (*United Bank v Akhtar* (1989)).
7. Unilateral variation of contract is impossible other than in an express term which is precise, clear and unambiguous on the issue – so an employer cannot claim the contract impliedly gives him/her the right to unilaterally vary terms (*Hayes v Securities and Facilities Division* (2000) CA).
8. Courts will not accept any ambiguous provision in contract acting to employee's detriment – following common law contract law principle of contra preferentum (*Skilton v T & K Home Improvements Ltd* (2000) CA).
9. It may also now be possible to apply the Unfair Contract Terms Act 1977 to contracts of employment (*Brigden v American Express Bank* (2000)).
10. Implied term of mutual trust and respect may also be used – there is precedent in the mobility clause cases that if express clause operates harshly or oppressively then the express term may be struck down by the implied term.

3.3.4 The advantages of express terms

1. There is possibly less room for dispute.
2. There is a consequent saving of time and money.
3. Express terms can be broadly stated so as to give greater scope to the employer.

3.3.5 Disadvantages

1. Express terms may be drafted too narrowly to cover employer's needs.
2. Express terms may be subject to narrow interpretation by the tribunal.

3.3.6 Conclusions

1. Since employer obliged to provide written statement then better to give written contract at commencement of employment.
2. Employers benefit by including broad terms.

3.4 COLLECTIVE AGREEMENTS

3.4.1 What are collective agreements?

1. These are made between employer's association (or employers) and trade unions, and they may define:
   - relationship between the two; and/or
   - terms and conditions for those within the agreement.
2. S1 statement often refers to collective agreements.
3. They have no effect unless incorporated into the contract.

3.4.2 Express incorporation

1. Most obvious way is express provision (*Jewell v Neptune Concrete* (1975)).
2. Express incorporation may mean contract need not be amended on each re-negotiation (*N.C.B. v Galley* (1958)).
3. S1 statement is common means of express incorporation (*Camden Exhibition & Display Ltd v Lynott* (1966)).
4. But to be incorporated, terms of collective agreement must represent intention of parties (*Alexander v Standard Telephone & Cables plc* (1990)).

Express incorporation
- Usually incorporated in s1 statement (*Camden Exhibition Display Ltd v Lynott*).
- May remove need to amend contract each time (*N.C.B. v Galley*).
- But must represent common intention (*Alexander v Standard Telephone & Cables plc*).
- Term may be procedural so not be incorporated (*Griffiths v Buckinghamshire CC*).
- If national and local agreements conflict, national usually prevail (*Loman & Henderson v Merseyside Transport Services Ltd*).
- But is a question of fact in each case (*Gascol Conversions v Mercer*).

COLLECTIVE AGREEMENTS

Non-union members
- Not settled.
- May be if incorporated (*Miller v Hamworthy Engineering Ltd*).

No strike clauses
- Covered by s180 Trade Union & Labour Relations (Consolidation) Act 1992.
- Only if it is in writing expressly, states it is incorporated, is accessible.

Termination
- Agreement if incorporated cannot be unilaterally varied or ended (*Robertson v British Gas Corporation*).
- Unilateral termination possible if contract allows for it (*Cadoux v Central Regional Council*).

Implied incorporation
- 'Officious bystanders test' applies.
- Some industries assume terms of union/management agreements (*McLea v Essex Line Ltd*).
- Long-term adherence may be sufficient to incorporate agreement (*Wilton v Peebles*).
- But employee only bound if knows of agreement and evidence of incorporation (*Joel v Camel Laird*).

WORKS RULES

Handbooks may mix contractual and non-contractual matter – distinction important as only non-contractual can be changed unilaterally.

ERA requires notice of some matters so strong evidence of contractual status (*Petrie v MacFisheries*).

But not everything in the rulebook is contractual (*Secretary of State for Employment v ASLEF (No 2)*).

Autocratic approach to rulebook may not be accepted (*Talbot v Hugh Fulton*).

Rules can be contractual despite their unilateral character (*Briggs v ICI*).

So generally rules will be contractual where expressly mentioned (*Singh v Lyons Maid Ltd*).

5. Collective agreement not always suitable for incorporation:

- as they relate to relationship between employer and TU (*British Leyland UK Ltd v McQuilken* (1978));
- term is procedural rather than conferring individual rights (*Griffiths v Buckinghamshire CC* (1994)).

6. If terms of national and local agreements conflict then:

- traditionally national agreement seen as binding (*Loman & Henderson v Merseyside Transport Services Ltd* (1967));
- more logical approach is most recent in time prevails (*Clift v West Riding CC* (1964));
- but it is a question of fact in each case which prevails (*Gascol Conversions v Mercer* (1974));
- local agreement adapts national one so may prevail.

3.4.3 Implied incorporation

1. Collective agreement may be incorporated by implication.
2. Which may be by 'officious bystander test'.
3. Some industries assume terms of union/management agreements (*McLea v Essex Line Ltd* (1933)).
4. Long-term adherence may be sufficient to incorporate the agreement (*Wilton v Peebles*).
5. But employee may only be bound if knows of agreement and evidence of incorporation (*Joel v Camel Laird* (1969)).

3.4.4 Collective agreements and non-union members

1. Legality of incorporation of collective agreements has not been properly considered by the courts – union may be agent of members but not of non-members.
2. So there is no settled position on non-unionists.
3. May bind non-unionist if expressly incorporated – or to a member of a different union (*Miller v Hamworthy Engineering Ltd* (1986)).

4. But if not expressly incorporated terms may not apply (*Singh v British Steel Corporation* (1974)).

5. So less easy to imply incorporation (*London Passenger Transport Board v Moscrop* (1942)).

6. Contract may allow variation by collective agreements.

3.4.5 No strike clauses

1. Now covered by s180 Trade Union & Labour Relations (Consolidation) Act 1992.

2. Provisions limiting industrial action only incorporated if:
- collective agreement is in writing;
- expressly states it is incorporated into contract and is actually incorporated;
- reasonably accessible in workplace in working hours.

3.4.6 Termination of collective agreements

1. Agreement if incorporated cannot be unilaterally varied or ended (*Robertson v British Gas Corporation* (1983)).

2. Though possible through lawful notice and agreement.

3. Unilateral termination is possible where contract allows for it (*Cadoux v Central Regional Council* (1986)).

4. Nothing illogical in accepting obligations which you can later terminate, employment contract is obvious example.

5. In practice employee may be forced to accept change.

3.5 WORKS RULES

3.5.1 The effects of work rules

1. May include disciplinary proceedings, health and safety, holidays, etc.

2. May be in booklet, on notice board, oral, etc.

3. Problem with handbooks is that they may mix contractual and non-contractual matter.

4. Distinction is important: contractual must be changed by agreement; non-contractual can be changed unilaterally.
5. So fact change in rule acts harshly is of no consequence (*Dryden v Greater Glasgow Health Board* (1992)).
6. ERA requires notice of some matters, so strong evidence of contractual status (*Petrie v MacFisheries* (1940)).
7. But not everything in the rulebook is contractual (*Secretary of State for Employment v ASLEF (No 2)* (1975)).
8. Some are classed as non-contractual administrative arrangements (*Peake v Automotive Products* (1977)).
9. Rules have been enforced even against blameless employees (*Jeffries v BP Tanker Co. Ltd* (1974)).
10. An autocratic approach to the rulebook may not be accepted (*Talbot v Hugh Fulton Ltd* (1975)).
11. Though rules can be contractual despite their unilateral character (*Briggs v ICI* (1968)).
12. So generally rules will be contractual where expressly mentioned (*Singh v Lyons Maid Ltd* (1975)).
13. Final analysis may turn on character of clause (*Anglia Regional Co-operative Society v O'Donnell* (1994)).

3.5.2 The importance of the job description

1. Common to have document detailing employee's duties.
2. This should be:
   - specific enough to identify precise details of work;
   - flexible enough to allow for variation.
3. Scope of contract is broader than range of duties and latter can be altered as long as still within former.

3.6 RESTRAINT OF TRADE CLAUSES

Protectable interests
Cannot merely prevent competition (*Strange v Mann*).
Can protect proprietary interests including:
● trade secrets (*Forster v Suggett*);
  – but not general knowledge of trade (*Herbert Morris v Saxelby*).
● client contact (*Fitch v Dewes*);
  – even if clients unknown to employee (*Plowman v Ash*);
  – but not people during the employment (*Gledhow Autoparts v Delaney*).
● against working for competitors unless forces employee to stay with employer
  (*Littlewoods Organisation Ltd v Harris*);
  – but must cover a protectable interest (*Commercial Plastics v Vincent*).
● solicitation of senior executives only (*Alliance Paper Group plc v Prestwich*);
  – but not employees generally (*Hanover Insurance Brokers Ltd v Schapiro*).

RESTRAINT OF TRADE CLAUSES

Construing restraint clauses
Employer cannot merely hide restraint behind other devices (*Bull v Pitney Bowes*).
But clause may be saved by construction (*Home Counties Dairies v Skilton*).
By severance or 'blue pencilling' if sense retained after removing clause (*Attwood v Lamont*).
Clause may not be too wide now when drafted to have effect regardless of reason for termination (*Rock Refrigeration v Jones Seward Refrigeration*).

Possible extent of restraint clauses
Restraint clauses are *prima facie* void.
Only valid if reasonable as between parties and in public interest.
Reasonable depends on:
– nature of business (*Forster v Suggett*);
– status of employee (*Plowman v Ash*);
– geographical extent (*Fitch v Dewes*);
– duration of restraint (*Home Counties Dairies Ltd v Skilton*).
Clause must not be too wide to cover protectable interests (*Fellowes v Fisher*).
Nor merely protect employer from competition (*Scully UK Ltd v Lee*).

3.6.1 Definition and character of a restraint clause

1. Defined as 'A legal device to attempt to balance two competing factors – employee's freedom to take employment as and when he wishes, and employer's interest in preserving certain aspects of his business from disclosure or exploitation by an employee, or, more usually, an ex-employee'.

2. Requires legal or contractual basis, so usually an express term – but can express agreement during or at end of contract (*RS Components Ltd v Irwin* (1974)).

3. Restrains employee on leaving to protect legitimate interests of employer – but may be applicable during contract i.e. as breach of fidelity.

4. Although express restraint clauses during employment are subject to normal challenges and controls (*Schroder Music Publishing Co. v Macaulay* (1974)).

5. And even if employee is paid to accept covenant it still must be justified to be valid (*Turner v Commonwealth & British Minerals Ltd* (2000)).

6. To protect freedom of contract, they are *prima facie* void.

3.6.2 Interests that can be protected

1. Employer cannot merely prevent employee from competing (*Strange v Mann* (1965)).

2. May protect only legitimate proprietary interests (*Herbert Morris Ltd v Saxelby* (1916)) including:

   (a) Trade secrets and confidential information.
   - Can protect against employee's disclosure of existing secrets/secret processes, or a well-guarded secret formula (*Forster v Suggett* (1918)).
   - But not mere general knowledge of trade or organisation (*Herbert Morris Ltd v Saxelby* (1916)).
   - And must also be able to show actual or perceived harm would result (*Jack Allen Sales and Service Ltd v Smith* (1999)).
   - Employer must in any case tell employee in precise terms what process is protected (*Lancashire Fires Ltd v SA Lyons & Co Ltd* (1999)).

   (b) The existing client connection.
   - To avoid 'poaching' of clients when trade means employee can build contact (*Fitch v Dewes* (1921)).

- Extent of client contact vital to determine validity of restraint (*Home Counties Dairies Ltd v Skilton* (1970)).
- So valid restraint where personal relationship built over many years (*International Consulting Services (UK) Ltd v Hart* (2000)).
- Restraint may be valid for customers unknown to employee and ones who had ceased business with the employer (*Plowman v Ash* (1964)).
- Not valid to extract a restraint from serving people who were not the employer's customers (*Gledhow Autoparts v Delaney* (1965)).
- Nor where the client contact is not recurrent (*Bowler v Lovegrove* (1921)).
- Nor where employment not of type where employee could gain confidence or trust of customer (*Attwood v Lamont* (1920)).

(c) Working for competitors.

- Generally courts do not give injunctions that merely compel a person to work for their existing employer (*Page One Records v Britton* (1967)).
- But if clause not such that it forces employee either to stay where s/he is or starve then it may be upheld (*Littlewoods Organisation Ltd v Harris* (1978)).
- But protection must operate in respect of protectable interests (*Commercial Plastics v Vincent* (1965)).

(d) Enticing away existing employees.

- A restraint preventing employees from soliciting other employees for another employer is generally void (*Hanover Insurance Brokers Ltd v Schapiro* (1994)).
- Agreements between employers having the effect of a restraint are void (*Kores v Kolok* (1959)).
- But courts may be prepared to allow non-solicitation clauses in respect of senior executives (*Ingham v ABC Contract Services* (1993) and *Alliance Paper Group plc v Prestwich* (1996)) and in solicitor's firms (*Wallace Bogan & Co. v Cove* (1997)).

3.6.3 The possible extent of restraint of trade clauses

1. A restraint is only valid if it is reasonable as between the parties, and in the public interest.
2. Reasonable means no wider than is sufficient to give employer protection of his legitimate interest – and the following may be taken into account:
    (a) nature of business (*Forster v Suggett* (1918));
    (b) status of employee (*Plowman v ASG* (1964));
    (c) geographical area covered by restraint (*Nordenfelt v Maxim Nordenfelt Co.* (1894)):
    - reasonable area is upheld (*Fitch v Dewes* (1924));
    - but generally restraint fails if area is unlimited (*Commercial Plastics Ltd v Vincent* (1965));
    - density of population may be a factor (*Mason v Provident Clothing & Supply Ltd* (1913));
    (d) duration for which restraint operates:
    - shorter the period more reasonable the restraint (*Home Counties Dairies Ltd v Skilton* (1970));
    - although short periods have been declared void (*Commercial Plastics Ltd v Vincent* (1965)).
3. What is reasonable will involve a complimentary analysis.
4. Ultimate test is whether restraint is too wide to cover protectable interests (*Fellowes & Son v Fisher* (1976)).
5. So clause seeking to 'protect' employer beyond competition unenforceable (*Scully UK Ltd v Lee* (1998)). As is a restraint preventing involvement 'in any capacity' (*Wincanton Ltd v Cranny* (2000)).

3.6.4 Interpreting and construing restraint clauses

1. If clause is too restrictive then it is void.
2. Nor will it be valid if employer attempts to hide restraint in other terms (*Stenhouse Australia Ltd v Phillips* (1974)).
3. Nor where employer uses other devices to achieve the same disincentive (*Bull v Pitney Bowes* (1966)).
4. A clause may be saved by construction (*Home Counties Dairies Ltd v Skilton* (1970)).

5. And also by severance or 'blue pencilling':
   - if some terms too wide and some not, then offending clause can be struck out (*Lucas v Mitchell* (1974));
   - but it must be capable of severance while still making sense (*Attwood v Lamont* (1970)).
6. A clause will not now be too wide because it is drafted to have effect regardless of reason for termination (*Rock Refrigeration v Jones Seward Refrigeration* (1996)).

3.6.5 Injunctive relief

1. The common remedy is an injunction.
2. Appropriate test is balance of convenience test in *American Cyanamid v Ethicon Ltd* (1975):
   - is there a serious issue to be tried?
   - would damages be an appropriate remedy (*Hollis & Co v Stocks* (2000))?
   - likelihood of claimant succeeding in full trial (*Lansing Linde Ltd v Kerr* (1991)).
3. Discretionary remedy, so only granted if appropriate and necessary (*GFI Group Inc. v Eaglestone* (1994)).
4. An injunction to enforce a contract of employment will not ordinarily be given – but may if restraint does not actually enforce performance (*Lumley v Wagner* (1852)).

3.7 GARDEN LEAVE CLAUSES

1. Where either side gives notice to terminate, employer will usually want employee to complete the notice and can insist on it.
2. If employee fails to do so an injunction is impossible – but employee might forfeit money owed during notice period.
3. Sometimes employer wants opposite, and because of type of position employee holds wants employee not to work during the notice period – this is 'garden leave'.

GARDEN LEAVE

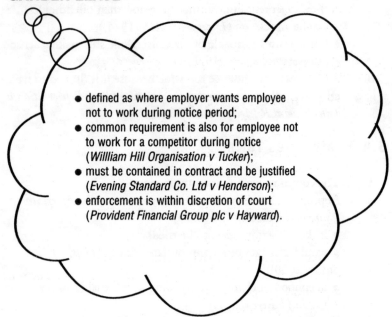

- defined as where employer wants employee not to work during notice period;
- common requirement is also for employee not to work for a competitor during notice (*Willliam Hill Organisation v Tucker*);
- must be contained in contract and be justified (*Evening Standard Co. Ltd v Henderson*);
- enforcement is within discretion of court (*Provident Financial Group plc v Hayward*).

4. During garden leave one common requirement of employer is for employee not to work for rival employer until notice period is ended – this is only possible if contract contains clause to that effect (*William Hill Organisation Ltd. v Tucker* (1999)).

5. For clause to be enforced employer must justify it in terms of length of notice, access to confidential information, connection with clients, and effect on remaining workforce (*Evening Standard Co. Ltd v Henderson* (1987)).

6. Where employee gives lawful notice enforcement of such clauses is still at court's discretion taking into account length of notice, whether employee is deprived of right to exercise skills, whether employer is protecting a legitimate interest (*Provident Financial Group plc v Hayward* (1989)).

7. The problem with garden leave clauses is that they can be easily abused, particularly if linked to very long notice periods, something the courts try to guard against.

8. But courts are more prepared to modify such clauses than they are with restraint clauses e.g. by reducing the period (*Symbian Ltd v Christensen* (2001)).

3.8 GRIEVANCE PROCEDURE

3.8.1 The causes of grievance

1. Grievances may be expressed about: management decisions, or about directors, or relationships with other employees, or conditions or external factors.

2. Common causes of grievance include:
- simple misunderstandings or communication breakdowns;
- unfair treatment;
- conflicts of interest;
- overly competitive behaviour and petty jealousies;
- personal frustration – commonly caused by being undervalued;
- poor performance in others;
- excessive and undue discipline;
- legal causes e.g. discrimination, harassment, victimisation.

3. Moaning is commonplace, taking a grievance procedure is not so it is important to take the employee's complaint seriously.

3.8.2 Statutory grievance procedures

1. Statutory Grievance Procedure introduced by Employment Act 2002 – based on minimum standards.

2. Stages in process:
- employee sends grievance in writing to employer;
- employer invites employee to at least one meeting (after full information given to other employee with right to respond);
- employer informs employee of decision in writing with reasons and right to appeal;
- employee informs if wishing to appeal;
- if so employer holds further meeting;
- employer informs employee of final decision.

3. Basic requirements of process:
   - each step to be completed without unreasonable delay;
   - reasonable time and place for meetings;
   - meetings conducted so all parties gain clear understanding;
   - higher management to hold appeals.

4. Right to representation now ensured by s10–15 Employment Relations Act 1999.
   - Can be by fellow worker or paid trade union official.
   - Right exists if hearing concerns 'performance of duty by employer in relation to a worker' – so applies to contractual duty e.g. underpayment of holidays or statutory duty e.g. health and safety complaint.
   - Can postpone hearing for representative to attend.
   - By new ACAS Code procedure must be held in good time.

5. Not providing grievance procedure can lead to successful claim of constructive dismissal (*W A Goold (Pearmak) Ltd v McConnell* (1995)).

6. An employee not using complete procedure may fail in constructive dismissal (*Witham v Hills Shopfitters*) unless justified by employer's breach (*Seligman & Latz Ltd v McHugh* (1979)).

7. Advantages of formal procedure include:
   - set time scale and predictable procedures;
   - can be devised by management and employees;
   - procedure will be constant even though staff change;
   - recorded so less room for misunderstanding;
   - allows employees to take grievance to highest level.

8. Disadvantages of formal procedure include:
   - lack of flexibility and development of set precedents;
   - ability of workforce to challenge management decisions;
   - possibility of linking grievance with ulterior 'political' aims;
   - will not necessarily remove cause of grievance;
   - failing to deal with grievances on the spot might allow resentment to fester.

9. By s31 and s32 Employment Act 2002 if statutory procedure is not followed, this can lead to possible fines on employer or loss of action in Employment Tribunal for employee.

3.9 DISCIPLINARY PROCEDURES

ACAS Code
- No legal force but following the code is evidence of good practice.
- Code says procedure should not be mere means of imposing sanctions but should:
  - emphasise and encourage improvements in individual conduct.
  - specify clearly and precisely rules necessary for efficient and safe performance of work.

Measures
Procedure only lawful if in contract. ACAS Code says should:
- be in writing;
- specify to whom it applies;
- provide speedy process;
- outline possible action;
- identify those with authority to take action;
- allow individual to hear complaint and answer it;
- allow for representation;
- no dismissal on first breach;
- ensure no action without full investigation;
- allow right of appeal.

DISCIPLINE

Warnings
No fixed form but ACAS Code says should be:
- informal oral warnings by supervisors for minor infringements;
- if disciplinary action, other than summary dismissal,
  - verbal warning;
  - written warning;
  - final written warning are all required.
- Power to issue warnings is contractual.
- Can deal with specific issues or may deal with conduct generally (*Donald Cook v Carter*).
- Warnings should always be:
  - given by a person with the appropriate authority;
  - in clear and precise form and language;
  - in writing if formal.
- Must use correct sequence (*Bendall v Paine & Betteridge*).

Hearings
- Not absolute requirement.
- Employer can determine composition.
- Purpose is to:
  - ascertain true facts;
  - allow employee to state his/her case.
- Must be conducted fairly – so should follow rules of natural justice:
  - employee must know allegations;
  - must be given opportunity to state own case;
  - must have own choice of representation – union rep. or fellow employee s10 Employment Relations Act 1999;
  - rule against bias applies.
- Judges differently to court hearings (*Ali v London Borough of Southwark*).
- Must have appeals procedure available.

3.9.1 The ACAS Code of Practice

1. Codes of practice are increasingly important because:
   - possibility of a claim of 'procedural unfairness';
   - tribunals increasingly encouraged to consider 'good industrial relations practice' in decisions;
   - much modern legislation refers to the use of Codes.

2. ACAS Codes have no legal force but may be evidence in tribunal of good or bad practice.

3. Discipline and dismissal originally in ACAS Code of Practice No 1: Disciplinary Practice and Procedures in Employment, now replaced by ACAS Code of Practice on Disciplinary and Grievance Procedures:
   - best practice suggests Procedure should be agreed;
   - by ERA s3 employees must be given written notice within two months of commencing employment;
   - code suggests 'Procedures should not be viewed primarily as a means of imposing sanctions. They should also be designed to emphasise and encourage improvements in individual conduct.' ' When drawing up rules the aim should be to specify clearly and concisely those necessary for the efficient and safe performance of work and for the maintenance of satisfactory relations within the workforce and between employees and management. Rules should not be so general as to be meaningless.'

4. New ACAS Code gives various advice on disciplinary proceedings and implementing procedures in ERA:
   - advice in paragraphs 19–25 on dealing with discipline, poor performance and absenteeism;
   - and misconduct – written warnings for relatively serious misconduct without need for oral procedure first (which the previous Code did not address).

3.9.2 Disciplinary measures

1. Disciplinary procedure is only lawful where employer has express or implied authority in the contract.
2. Or employee may seek to have unlawful act overturned.
3. ACAS Code states that a disciplinary procedure should:
   - be in writing;
   - specify to whom it applies;
   - provide for matters to be dealt with quickly;
   - indicate the disciplinary actions which may be taken;
   - specify levels of management with authority to take different action – immediate superiors must not have the power to dismiss;
   - provide for individuals to be informed of complaints against them, and to be given the opportunity to state their case before decisions are reached;
   - allow individuals the right to be accompanied by a TU rep. or a fellow employee;
   - ensure that, but for gross misconduct, employees are not dismissed for a first breach of discipline;
   - ensure no action taken without full investigation;
   - ensure explanations are given for any penalty imposed;
   - provide a right of appeal together with specified procedures for appeal.

3.9.3 Disciplinary hearings

1. Hearings are not absolute requirement but sound policy.
2. Generally reference to hearings found in employer's disciplinary procedure – but *ad hoc* hearings possible.
3. Composition of a hearing is within the employer's power to determine – but it can be by collective agreement.
4. There are two significant functions of a hearing:
   - means of ascertaining true facts of incident(s) leading to requirement for discipline to be imposed;
   - allows employee to state his/her case or to mitigate.

5. Hearings must be conducted according to fair practice – so they should tend to follow the rules of natural justice:
- employee should know the details of the allegations
  - (i) so be able to prepare a case;
  - (ii) no unfair dismissal if allegations clear and obvious (*Fuller v Lloyds Bank plc* (1991)).
- employee should be given opportunity to state a case
  - (i) although employee need not be present;
  - (ii) and hearing unnecessary if employee accepts allegations (*Sutherland v Sonat Offshore (UK) Inc.*).
- should have access to representation of choice
  - (i) now in s10 Employment Relations Act 1999;
  - (ii) can be fellow worker or trade union representative;
  - (iii) person accompanying worker can take full part but not answer on behalf of employee;
  - (iv) right arises on a formal warning, other action, or confirmation of a warning issued by other action;
  - (v) so if employer merges investigation and discipline (s)he is bound to allow representation or no further action after informal stage;
  - (vi) can postpone so representative can attend.
- rule against bias also applies – significant to appeals.

6. Disciplinary hearings judged differently to court procedure (*Ali v London Borough of Southwark* (1988)).

7. Must have appeals procedure available:
- required by paragraph 10(k) of ACAS Code;
- but no particular form is required;
- absence of appeal does not automatically mean dismissal was unfair;
- but any appeal procedure must be fair;
- though need not follow court procedures (*Rowe v Radio Rentals* (1982));
- appeals may be 'unnecessary and inappropriate' (*McLaren v NCB* (1988)).

3.9.4 Disciplinary warnings

1. A common feature of modern disciplinary procedures.

2. No fixed procedure required.

3. Paragraph 12 of ACAS Code suggests there should be:
- 'informal oral warnings by supervisors for minor infringements', and
- if disciplinary action, other than summary dismissal, required then following should apply:
  - (i) **verbal warning** for minor misconduct – written note of warning kept on personnel files for specified period, employee informed of reason for warning, given chance of hearing;
  - (ii) **written warning** for more serious misconduct or repeated misconduct;
  - (iii) **final written warning** for serious misconduct or failure to respond to former warnings – this warning should identify the possibility of suspension or dismissal.

4. Presence or absence of warning system important in determining fairness or otherwise of dismissal.

5. Power to issue warnings is usually contractual – so should be identified in 'works rules'.

6. Employer should set procedure in advance and conform to it at all stages in process.

7. Fact final written warning issued does not automatically make dismissal next step (*Newall's Insulation v Blakeman* (1976)).

8. Warnings can deal with specific issues or may deal with conduct generally (*Donald Cook v Carter* (1977)).

9. A tribunal will not scrutinise choice of warning – but unfair dismissal may result from choosing a process seen as 'manifestly inappropriate in all the circumstances' (*Co-operative Retail Services Ltd v Lucas*).

10. Warnings can be for any period – but must last for their stated time (*Bevan Ashford v Malin* (1995)).

11. Warnings should always be:
- given by a person with the appropriate authority;

- in clear and precise form and in precise and firm language;
- in writing if formal.

12. A system of warnings must always be used in its correct sequence (*Bendall v Paine & Betteridge* (1973)).
13. Though it is sometimes possible to miss out stages where seriousness of breach of discipline warrants it.

3.9.5 Statutory Dismissal and Disciplinary Procedure (SDDP)

1. New standard procedure introduced in Employment Act 2002 (based on minimum standards).
2. Stages where dismissal contemplated:
   - employer sends written statement of circumstances leading to contemplating discipline by dismissal with grounds and time for employee to respond;
   - disciplinary meeting held (with no prior action except necessary suspension);
   - employer informs employee of decision in writing and notifies right to appeal;
   - employee informs of wish to appeal if (s)he wishes;
   - second meeting held – possible to dismiss before this meeting;
   - employer informs of final decision.
3. Same general requirements as for statutory grievance procedure.
4. Special rules for summary dismissal for gross misconduct:
   - employer sends written details and notifies of right to appeal;
   - employee informs employer if wishes to appeal;
   - meeting held;
   - written decision given to employee.
5. Possible to disapply statutory procedure in some circumstances, e.g. in large scale redundancies or unofficial strike action etc.

CHAPTER 4

IMPLIED TERMS

Incorporating implied terms
- Measured by 'officious bystander test' (*Shirlaw v Southern Foundries*).
- Or by custom if 'certain, notorious, and reasonable' (*Sagar v Ridehaigh*).
- Original justification was needed for business efficacy (*The Moorcock*).
- Now is 'necessary incident of definite category of contractual relationship' (*Scally v Southern Health & Social Services Board*).
- Effect on express terms is disputable – compare *United Bank v Akhtar* and *Rank Xerox Ltd v Churchill*.
- Now terms can be implied despite intent of parties (*Johnstone v Bloomsbury Health Authority*).

IMPLIED TERMS

Employer's duties
To pay wages (*Way v Latilla*).
To provide work for e.g. actors, pieceworkers etc. (*Herbert Clayton & Jack Waller Ltd v Oliver*).
Take reasonable care of employee:
- provide safe system, plant, premises, colleagues (*Wilson & Clyde Coal Co. v English*);
- not cause psychiatric harm (*Walker v Northumberland*);
- But no duty to property (*Deyong v Shenburn*).
To indemnify for all reasonable expenses.
To give mutual trust and respect:
- protect from sexual harrassment (*Bracebridge Engineering v Darby*);
- not to be deliberately provocative (*Donovan v Invicta Airways*).
To protect confidentiality (*Dalgleish v Lothian & Borders Policy Board*).
To deal properly with grievances (*W A Goold (Pearmark) Ltd v McConnell*).

Employee's duties
To obey lawful (*Morrish v Henlys*) and reasonable instructions (*Ottoman Bank Ltd v Chakarian*).
To exercise care and skill:
- complete work competently (*Harmer v Cornelius*);
- protect employer's property (*Superlux v Plaidstead*).
To adapt to necessary changes (*Cresswell v Board of Inland Revenue*).
To give faithful service:
- not harm employer's business (*Secretary of State for Employment v ASLEF*);
- not to compete with employer (*Hivac v Park Royal Scientific Instruments*);
- must disclose misdeeds of colleagues (*Sybron Corporation v Rochem*);
- not to misuse confidential information (*Faccenda Chicken v Fowler*);
- not to make a secret profit (*Boston Deep Sea Fishing & Ice Co. v Ansell*).

4.1 THE PROCESS OF IMPLYING TERMS

4.1.1 Implied terms

1. Prevalent throughout contract law and employment law.
2. Court implies term to cover contingency where contract fails to e.g. implied mobility clauses (*Stevenson v Teeside Bridge & Engineering Ltd* (1971)).
3. Terms are also implied by statute and by EU law.

4.1.2 The process of incorporating implied terms

1. Done by courts in hindsight following dispute – so subject to disagreement of parties.
2. Original justification needed to give business efficacy to contract (*The Moorcock* (1889)).
3. Measured by 'officious bystander test : MacKinnon LJ in *Shirlaw v Southern Foundries Ltd* (1939).
4. Or by custom if certain, notorious and reasonable (*Sagar v Ridehalgh* (1931) but compare with *Samways v Swan Hunter Shipbuilders* (1975)).
5. May now be based on what is reasonable on evidence of relationship between the parties and what has happened since the employment began (*Mears v Safecar Security Ltd* (1983)).
6. So parties would probably have agreed if they were being reasonable (*Courtaulds Northern Spinning Ltd v Sibson* (1988) compare with *Prestwick Circuits Ltd v McAndrew* (1991)).
7. Effect on express terms is disputable, compare *United Bank v Akhtar* (1989) with *Rank Xerox Ltd v Churchill* (1988).
8. Efficacy has been widened to include a term which is a necessary incident of a definite category of contractual relationship (*Scally v Southern Health & Social Services Board* (1991)) and Lord Reid in *Sterling Engineering Co. Ltd v Patchett* (1955).
9. Categories of implied terms not fixed but expanding: employer owes employee respect and trust, and should not treat employee arbitrarily or vindictively (*Robinson v*

Crompton Parkinson Ltd (1978)), (*Gardiner Ltd v Beresford* (1978)), (*Warner v Barbers Stores* (1978)).

10. Some terms implied irrespective of intention of parties due to importance, and may override express terms (*Johnstone v Bloomsbury Health Authority* (1991)).

4.2 THE IMPLIED DUTIES OF EMPLOYERS

1. To pay wages (*Way v Latilla* (1937)).

2. To provide work:
- there is no absolute 'right to work' (*Collier v Sunday Referee Publishing Co. Ltd* (1940));
- but see Denning MR in *Langton v AUEW* (1974);
- and in certain employment e.g. acting, it may be vital (*Herbert Clayton & Jack Waller Ltd v Oliver* (1930));
- and for highly-skilled professionals, pieceworkers and those paid by commission.

3. To take reasonable care of the employee:
- a contractual duty of care and a tortious one (*Tai Hing Cotton Mill Ltd v Chong Hing Bank Ltd* (1986));
- must provide safe system, premises, colleagues, plant (*Wilson & Clyde Coal Co. v English* (1938));
- and duty not to cause psychiatric harm or undue stress (*Walker v Northumberland CC* (1995));
- but no duty to care for the employee's property (*Deyong v Shenburn* (1946));
- nor to care for the employee's general economic wellbeing (*Crossley v Faithful & Gould Holdings* (2004));
- nor to provide personal accident insurance (*Reid v Rush & Tompkins Group* (1989));
- but there is a duty not to give negligent references (*Spring v Guardian Assurance plc* (1994)).

4. The duty to indemnify:
- applies to all expenses necessarily incurred in the course of employment e.g. travel, lodging;

- but not legal proceedings (*Gregory v Ford* (1951)).

5. The duty of mutual trust and respect:
  - must protect from sexual harassment (*Bracebridge Engineering Ltd v Darby* (1990));
  - Must not unilaterally change pay or status (*Arden v Bradley* (1994));
  - nor criticize in front of peers (*IOW Tourist Board v Coombes* (1976));
  - nor swear at domestic staff (*Wilson v Racher* (1974));
  - nor be deliberately provocative (*Donovan v Invicta Airways* (1970));
  - so must treat all employees fairly and evenly and not exclude individuals from benefits given to all others (*BG plc v   O'Brien* (2001));
  - and on dismissal implied term is extended to include all pre-dismissal conduct (*Eastwood v Magnox Electric plc; McCabe v Cornwall County Council* (2004)).

6. The duty of confidentiality:
  - employer may not pass on information relevant only to the employment and not public knowledge (*Dalgleish v Lothian & Borders Police Board* (1991)).

7. The duty to deal properly with grievances:
  - must have effective procedure and chance of redress (*W.A. Goold (Pearmak)) Ltd v McConnel* (1995)).

4.3 THE IMPLIED DUTIES OF EMPLOYEES

1. Duty to obey lawful and reasonable instructions:
  - originates with master/servant rules and masters right to chastise – but now more to do with co-operation;
  - dismissal is fair if lawful or reasonable orders refused (*UK Atomic Energy Authority v Claydon* (1974));
  - the refusal not its manner is the breach (*Pepper v Webb* (1969));

- employee need not obey unlawful orders (*Morrish v Henlys Ltd* (1973));
- nor unreasonable ones (*Ottoman Bank Ltd v Chakarian* (1930), contrast with *Walmsley v Udec Refrigerators Ltd* (1972));
- reasonable may be measured against good industrial relations (*Payne v Spook Erection Ltd* (1984));
- refusal may not necessarily justify dismissal (*Wilson v IDR Construction Ltd* (1975), compare with *Robinson v Flitwick Frames Ltd* (1975)).

2. The duty to exercise care and skill:
   - must undertake work competently using reasonable care and skill (*Harmer v Cornelius* (1858));
   - and take care of employer's property (*Superlux v Plaidstead* (1958)).

3. The duty to adapt:
   - unless changes are so fundamental as to change job, employee should adapt to change (*Cresswell v Board of Inland Revenue* (1984));
   - so a refusal to attend training is breach (*Connor v Halfords Ltd* (1972)).

4. The duty of faithful service or fidelity:
   - not to harm employer's business (*Secretary of State for Employment v ASLEF* (1972) and *Dalton v Burtons Gold Medal Biscuit Co.* (1974));
   - not to compete, courts dislike prohibiting spare-time activities unless they harm the employer (*Hivac Ltd v Park Royal Scientific Instruments Ltd* (1946));
   - to disclose misdeeds of colleagues, compare *Bell v Lever Bros* (1932) with *Sybron Corporation v Rochem* (1983);
   - not to misuse confidential information:
     (i) applies strictly to current employees (*Foster v Scaffolding Ltd* (1973));
     (ii) but is limited to trade secrets and trade connection with ex-employees (*Faccenda Chicken Ltd v Fowler* (1986));
     (iii) poaching clients is a straightforward breach (*Sanders v Parry* (1967)).

- employee inventions traditionally owned by employer if made in course of employment (*British Syphon Co. Ltd v Homewood* (1956)) but see s39 Patents Act 1977 & Copyright Designs and Patents Act 1988;
- not to make a secret bribe, commission or profit (*Boston Deep Sea Fishing & Ice Co. v Ansell* (1888)).

CHAPTER 5

STATUTORY PROTECTIONS

Time off for ante-natal care
- Must be allowed if appointment advised by doctor, midwife, health visitor.
- Should be paid time off.

Additional maternity leave
- One year qualifying period in employment.
- Allows right to return to same or broadly similar job up to 26 weeks after the birth.

Ordinary maternity leave
- Requires proper notification to the employer, or a premature birth;
- Period is for 26 weeks.
- Paid by statutory maternity pay or contractual pay if available.

MATERNITY

Pregnancy related dismissals
- These are automatically unfair (*Dekker, Webb v EMO Air Cargo*).

Statutory maternity pay
- Paid for a maximum of 26 weeks.
- Must be employed for 26 weeks before leave date to qualify.
- Paid by employer at rate of 90% of pay for six weeks, then on a flat rate.

5.1 MATERNITY

5.1.1 Background

1. An area subject to radical change in recent years:
   - in the mechanics of payment;
   - changes to comply with Directive 92/85 on HASAW;
   - changes on the right to dismiss pregnant women;
   - to leave period to bring in line with pay period;
   - and to comply with Directive 96/34 on parental leave.

2. The area has been confusing because:
   - UK law differed from EC law so had to change;
   - it did so by grafting new rights on top of old ones.

5.1.2 Time off for ante-natal care

1. S55 ERA gives right not to be unfairly denied time to keep appointments if advised by doctor, midwife, health visitor.
2. Right arises from moment appointment is made.
3. But unavailable in the case of:
   - those not working under a contract of employment;
   - those working outside of UK;
   - sharefisherwomen, members of the constabulary.
4. Right includes normal payment at usual rate – s56 ERA.
5. To claim woman must show refusal was unreasonable:
   - complaint must be made within three months of refusal;
   - tribunal can make declaration/award compensation – s57 ERA.

5.1.3 Suspension on maternity grounds

1. Management of Health and Safety at Work (Amendment) Regulations 1994 oblige employers to carry out a risk assessment on pregnant women. If none is carried out then a civil action for discrimination is possible (*Day v T Pickles Farm Ltd* (1999)).

2. s66 ERA requires employer to suspend women where:
   - there is a risk to an expectant or recent mother and it is impossible to alter her work;
   - she works nights and doctor/midwife certifies it unsafe.
3. By s67 must offer suitable alternative work if available:
   - failure to offer gives rise to claim for compensation;
   - unreasonable refusal to accept an offer may result in losing right to pay during suspension.
4. By s68 must pay woman normal rate while suspended.
5. Rights do not require qualifying period of employment.

5.1.4 The right to maternity leave

1. By s72 ERA employer may not allow woman to return within two weeks of birth (called 'compulsory maternity leave') – subject to fines.
2. Irrespective of service woman is entitled to 'ordinary maternity leave' (except armed forces, police, sharefisherwomen).
3. A woman must: notify employer of pregnancy, expected week of confinement, provide doctor's certificate if requested – s75, and of date leave begins (not more than 11 weeks before confinement), notice 15 weeks before leaving, and if notification by normal methods impossible should notify in writing as soon as reasonably practicable.
4. Leave commences on date notified, or four weeks before confinement, or day after birth, whichever is earliest.
5. Leave period is 26 weeks from that date, extended by four weeks with sick note or early return with seven days notice.
6. Leave commencement date is automatic trigger if:
   - birth is premature and before expected date maternity leave is to commence; or
   - employee is absent from work wholly or partly due to pregnancy or childbirth after beginning of fourth week before expected date of confinement.
7. There is no basic entitlement to pay during leave:
   - but all other contractual benefits available;
   - if no paid leave Statutory Maternity Pay available.

8. Leave period also counts towards continuity.
9. Dismissal during leave is automatically unfair – except in redundancies if suitable alternative work offered.
10. Woman can exercise her contractual rights if better.

5.1.5 The right to a maternity payment

1. This is now a statutory scheme – Statutory Maternity Pay:
   - employer pays this for a maximum of 26 weeks;
   - payment is recouped from NI payments at the rate of 92% or 100% plus compensation for small firms.
2. Two pay scales – six weeks at 90% of earnings then flat rate:
   - if more than one employer both pay a part;
   - payment starts in week after leave commences;
   - maximum pay period is 26 weeks starting any time after eleven weeks before confinement up to one week after;
   - there can be no payment after returning to work.
3. Woman has to qualify for SMP – so:
   - must be paying class 1 NI contributions;
   - and employed for 26 weeks prior to qualifying week;
   - with earnings above lower level rate for NI payment;
   - must give employer medical certificate of expected date of confinement and 28 days notice of leave date;
   - must have reached eleventh week before confinement, or given birth.
4. If not eligible may be eligible for Maternity Allowance:
   - paid directly by the benefits agency;
   - woman has to show that she:
     (i) is pregnant and has reached eleventh week before confinement;
     (ii) was employed or self-employed for 26 weeks in 66 prior to confinement;
     (iii) paid 26 weeks Class 1 or 2 NI in 66 weeks;
     (iv) she is not entitled to SMP.
5. It is paid for a maximum 26 weeks at a flat rate.

5.1.6 Additional maternity leave and the right to return

1. Traditional rules modified in 1993 to accommodate 'leave'.
2. Now called 'additional maternity leave' and a woman is entitled to it if she is entitled to 'ordinary maternity leave' and was continuously employed for 26 weeks up to the fourteenth week before confinement.
3. Gives further 26 weeks leave after OML ends (counts towards continuous employment).
4. No obligation to inform employer of date of return from OML:
   - this contrasts sharply with previous law that required a strict set of notice requirements;
   - employer must inform of date for return within 28 days (and in AML 28 days from receiving notice of taking AML);
   - employer though can postpone this date for 4 weeks;
   - as can the woman with a doctor's note;
   - woman can still change her mind and not return.
5. Right to return from OML should be to same (but not necessarily identical) role and no less favourable role:
   - from AML return must be on no less favourable terms but to 'suitable alternative work' where impracticable to return to old job.
6. Redundancy in this time for reasons of pregnancy is automatically unfair:
   - though not if it is by fair selection e.g. LIFO;
   - there are exemptions for small businesses in s96.

5.1.7 Dismissal on grounds of pregnancy

1. Automatically unfair if reason of dismissal is:
   - pure pregnancy (*Brown v Stockton BC* (1988));
   - contract terminated after leave when woman asserted maternity rights;
   - birth of a child;

- statutory restriction e.g. HASAW;
- suitable alternative work available but not offered.

2. Is also against EU law (*Webb v EMO Air Cargo (UK) Ltd* (1995) and *Gillespie v Northern Health & Social Services Board* (1996)).
3. If the woman is fairly dismissed or made redundant then leave ends on date of termination.

5.2 PARENTAL LEAVE, DEPENDANT CARE LEAVE, ADOPTION LEAVE

1. Now available following Council Directive 96/34.
2. UK implemented Directive in Schedule 4 Employment Relations Act 1999 – introduced provision in Maternity and Parental Leave Regulations 1999–2001 in Reg. 13.
3. Regulation has a number of basic qualifications:
   - either parent seeking leave must have at least one year's continuous service with the employer;
   - party claiming must be a named parent on birth certificate of child under five born after 15th December 1999;
   - or is the legal adopted parent of the child;
   - or has acquired parental responsibility for the child under Children Act 1989.
4. Regulations operate in following ways:
   - allows 13 weeks leave lasting until child's fifth birthday or fifth anniversary of adoption;
   - right is an individual one so is available to both parents;
   - if child suffers from a disability parents can spread the leave until child is 18;
   - parents using provision are still covered by contract rights during leave, and have right to return to work;
   - any dismissal for reasons purely to do with the leave will be automatically unfair;

- regulations anticipate that employers and employees might negotiate their own detailed agreements concerning the operation of the scheme.

5. Later Regulations, to comply with Directive, include provisions for time off to care for dependant relatives e.g. parents, partners and children.

6. Provides absolute entitlement for time off:
   - to help when a dependant is ill, injured, or is assaulted;
   - to make arrangements for provision of care for a dependant who is ill or injured;
   - in consequence of the death of a dependant;
   - because of unexpected disruption to the care arrangements of a dependant;
   - to deal with issues involving a child of the employee arising in an educational establishment.

7. Now under Paternity and Adoption Leave Regulations 2002 employee may take 'ordinary adoption leave' and 'additional adoption leave' with broadly the same qualifications and rights as maternity leave.

5.3 WAGES

5.3.1 The right to wages at common law

1. Obligation to pay wages is basically contractual, though many rules on payment of wages derive from statute.

2. No need for set wage e.g. could be paid commission.

3. Employee can recover on *quantum meruit*, sum earned if:
   - contract silent on wages (*Upton R.D.C. v Powell* (1942));
   - terms are vague (*Way v Latilla* (1937));
   - for pay other than wages (*Powell v Braun* (1954)).

4. Although right to *quantum* may be lost where the obligation is entire and work is unfinished (*Cutter v Powell* (1795) but see *Hoenig v Isaacs* (1952)).

Common law right to wages

- Right is basically contractual.
- *Quantum meruit* is possible e.g. where terms are vague (*Way v Latilla*).
- Can refuse pay where work not performed is quantifiable (*Miles v Wakefield MDC*) or pay nothing where employee has frustrated rather than advanced employer's business (*BT plc v Ticehurst*).
- Employees must return overpayments of wages (*Avon CC v Howlett*).

Payment during sickness

- No common law right (*Mears v Safecar Security Ltd*).
- Now under Statutory Sick Pay Act 1994 employer must pay SSP.
- Pay is for up to 28 weeks, less first three days, if day of claim is:
  - a period of incapacity;
  - within period of entitlement;
  - when employee would have worked.
- Disqualified if:
  - three months or less fixed term;
  - employment has not commenced;
  - 28 weeks has expired;
  - sickness during trade dispute.
- Contract rights prevail if better.

WAGES

Deductions from pay

Legitimate deductions in s13 ERA:
- authorised by statute;
- authorised by employee in writing;
- authorised by contract.

Exemptions in s14:
- overpayment of wages;
- disciplinary under statute;
- unpaid taxes;
- union subscriptions;
- court orders.

Wages include non-contractual payments (*Kent Management Services v Butterfield*).
But not expenses (*London Borough of Southwark v O'Brien*).
Payment in lieu of notice is not wages so is actionable in court (*Delaney v Staples*).

Minimum Wage Act

Minimum Wage Act 1998 applies to:
- employees;
- personal service but not under a business;
- agency and out workers;
- foreign workers;
- others authorised by Secretary of State.

But not volunteers, trainees and apprentices, au-pairs and nannies.
Based on minimum rates for:
- 18–21;
- 22 and over;
- trainees over 22.

Dismissal for asserting right to minimum pay is automatically unfair.

5. S8 Employment Rights Act 1996 gives workers (except share fishermen or merchant seamen) right to itemised pay statement, showing gross and net pay and variables.

6. An action on wages can be for unilateral changes in conditions (*Burdett-Coutts v Hertfordshire C.C.* (1984)).

7. Agreement of 'no work no pay' is possible if employee refuses to do work required by contract (*Cresswell v Board of Inland Revenue* (1984)):
   - can refuse to pay for work not performed where quantifiable (*Miles v Wakefield M.D.C.* (1987) and *Royle v Trafford* (1984)).
   - or pay nothing – by implied duty on employee with discretion how to do work to advance not frustrate employer's business (*BT plc v Ticehurst* (1992)).

8. Employee is obliged to return overpayments of wages:
   - since they are mistakes of fact and so restitution applies (*Avon C.C. v Howlett* (1983));
   - if employee knows of mistake and fails to return can be liable for theft (*A.G.'s Reference* (No 1 of 1983).

9. Breach of a term by late payment or non-payment only allows employee to repudiate if non-payment is deliberate and intentional and directed at employee (*Cantor, Fitzgerald International v Callaghan* (1999)).

10. Complaint about wages is to courts – subject to changes in Wages Act 1986 diverting claims to tribunal.

5.3.2 Payments during sickness

1. No automatic common law right to pay during sickness:
   - so at common law is governed by express terms;
   - so if no express term, then no presumption sick pay should be paid. Though all facts of case must be considered (*Mears v Safecar Security Ltd* (1982)).
   - in absence of conclusive evidence tribunal cannot invent term (*Eagland v British Telecommunications plc* (1992)).

2. Common law less significant since Statutory Sick Pay created in Social Security & Housing Benefits Act 1982:
   - because of administrative inefficiency in prior system;
   - since modified in Social Security Contributions and Benefits Act 1992 & Statutory Sick Pay Act 1994.
3. Scheme now is employer must pay sick employee up to 28 weeks (but not first three days), at standard rate.
4. Employee may be eligible for long-term incapacity benefits from state after those 28 weeks.
5. Three qualifying conditions:
   (i) Day payment is sought, must be 'period of incapacity for work' (disease or mental or physical disablement which renders him/her incapable of doing any work).
   (ii) Day of claim must be within a period of entitlement.
   (iii) Day in question must be a qualifying day (i.e. a day on which the employee would have worked).
6. Employee is disqualified from receiving payment where:
   - work is for a three months or less fixed term;
   - employee has not yet started work;
   - 28 weeks has expired;
   - sickness occurs during a trade dispute.
7. Method of notification is as agreed in contract subject to rules on self certification.
8. In the absence of an agreed time statutory period of seven days applies (+ 90 day extension with good cause).
9. SSP does not alter contractual obligations.

5.3.3 Deductions from pay

1. Statutory protection originally in Truck Acts 1831 & 1896.
2. Repealed in Wages Act 1986 (more about non-cash pay).
3. But rules on deductions extended to include all workers and now in ss 13 – 27 ERA '96.
4. S13 identifies the only legitimate deductions:
   - those authorised by statute (tax, NI, attachment of earnings orders);

- those authorised by employee in writing before deduction made (*Potter v Hunt Contracts Ltd* (1992));
- those authorised by contract of employment.

5. Deduction must be justified in fact as well as authorised (*Fairfield v Skinner* (1993)).

6. In general a remedy is sought in a tribunal under s23.

7. By s14 some deductions exempt so recourse is to courts:
   - overpayment of wages or expenses;
   - disciplinary proceedings held under statutory provision;
   - statutory rule to pass to public body (unpaid taxes);
   - payments to a third party (e.g. TU subscriptions);
   - in respect of industrial action;
   - court or tribunal orders requiring payment to employer.

8. Wages defined in s27 as 'any sums payable to worker by his employer in connection with his employment':
   - so wide enough to include non-contractual payments (*Kent Management Services Ltd v Butterfield* (1992));
   - but not expenses, however generous (*London Borough of Southwark v O'Brien* (1996)).

9. Deductions defined in s13(3) 'total amount of wages paid is less than total amount of wages properly payable':
   - covers total failure to pay (*Delaney v Staples* (1991));
   - and methods used to hide a deduction (*McCree v London Borough of Tower Hamlets* (1992));
   - and a reduction in work leading to reduction in pay counts as a deduction (*International Packaging Corporation (UK) Ltd v Balfour* (2003)).

10. Payments in lieu of notice are not wages so are not deductions under Act so are actionable in court not tribunal (*Delaney v Staples* (1991)).

11. And an action on a PILON clause has been held to be one for debt (*Cerberus Software Ltd v Rowley* (2001)) so employer dismissing wrongfully will be liable for all payment in lieu of notice.

12. One possible problem is assessing ways wages are apportioned on termination (*Thames Water Utilities v Reynolds* (1996)).

13. Under s17 special rules exist in retailing for recovery for stock shortages.

5.3.4 The minimum wage

1. Not a new concept, originally in Conditions of Employment and National Arbitration Order 1940, to enforce collective agreements for specific trades.
   - Extended by Schedule 11 Employment Protection Act 1975 giving action for paying less favourable wages than for comparable workers in same industry.
   - Wages Councils regulated many low paid jobs, but abolished in Trade Union Reform and Employment Rights Act 1993.
2. National Minimum Wage Act 1998 introduced for:
   - employees working under a contract of employment;
   - those under a verbal or written contract to provide personal services but not in the course of a business;
   - agency workers, and home workers unless genuinely self-employed;
   - foreign workers working here, British working abroad;
   - Secretary of State may extend to other people.
3. Certain groups are currently not covered by the Act:
   - genuine volunteers;
   - trainees aged 18, apprentices aged 19–26 in first year of apprenticeship;
   - live in au-pairs, nannies and companions where no deduction from wages for accommodation and food and domestic chores are genuinely shared.
4. Based on single minimum rate with no variation for area from October 2004:
   - £4.10 for those between 18 and 21;
   - £4.85 for those aged 22 and over;
   - £3.00 for those between 16 and 17.
5. Employer must keep records, and prove minimum wage is met if employee complains to Court or Tribunal that it has not. Compensation payment of 80 times hourly rate payable to employee if employer in default.
6. Dismissal for asserting right to minimum pay automatically unfair.
7. Criminal penalties also available to enforcement officers.

5.4 GUARANTEE PAYMENTS

1. Applies during lay off and in short time.
2. A lay off is defined as a week when an employee receives no pay due to him/her under the contract of employment.
3. Short time is defined as a week when an employee receives less than half the pay entitled under the contract.
4. Both situations may eventually lead to redundancy rights.
5. Either may occur because of lack of orders, recession etc. – common in construction industry, shipbuilding etc.
6. There is a confused common law position.
   - Lay off with pay is lawful – unless a right to work exists.
   - Without pay is not (*Devonland v Rosser & Sons* (1906)).
   - But may be when it is beyond the employer's control (*Browning v Crumlin Valley Collieries* (1926)).
   - Problem can be resolved by provisions in the contract and very often will be by collective agreement.
7. Uncertainty of common law and need for employee to maintain income have led to development of guarantee payments under statute:
   - developed in the Employment Protection Act 1975 and now in Employment Rights Act 1996 ss 28–35;
   - designed to encourage employer to act responsibly so any contractual payments are set off against statutory scheme and employers can gain exemption.
8. Employees will qualify for a payment:
   - with one month's consecutive service;
   - for a workless normal workday;
   - the reason is a diminution of work or other event affecting normal work of business.
9. There is no entitlement where:
   - there is a trade dispute;
   - suitable alternative employment has been refused;
   - employee ignores reasonable attendance requirement.
10. Amount of guarantee payment is normal working hours x guaranteed hourly rate, subject to statutory maximum.
11. Scheme subject to tax, job seekers allowance unavailable.
12. Complaint must go to tribunal in three months.

CHAPTER 6

DISCRIMINATION

The equality clause and comparitor
- Woman's contract should be no less favourable than man's – and should contain any beneficial clause in man's.
- Comparison must be with man in same or associate employment – who may precede woman (*MacArthys v Smith*) or succeed woman (*Diocese of Hallam Trustees v Connaughten*).

Classes of claim in Equal Pay Act 1970
Like work under s1(4):
- must be broadly similar (*Sorbie v Trust House Forte*).

Work rated equivalent under s1(5):
- follows objective job evaluation study (*Bromley v H & J Quick*);
- result of study must be implemented (*Arnold v Beecham Group Ltd*).

Work of equal value:
- inserted in Amendment Regulations 1983 after infringement proceedings against UK for failure to implement directive 75/117;
- again based on a job evaluation study – but ordered by tribunal and carried out by ACAS – first successful claim in *Hayward v Camel Laird Shipbuilders*.

EQUAL PAY

Avoiding equal pay claims
Difference may be justified by a 'genuine material factor' – s1(3) e.g.:
- location (*NAAFI v Varley*);
- different responsibilities (*Capper Pass v Allan*);
- inconvenience (*Calder v Rowntree Mackintosh*);
- different productivity (*Jenkins v Kingsgate Clothing*);
- economic necessity (*Rainey v Greater Glasgow HB*);
- red circling (*Methven v Cow Industries*);

But not:
- reducing wage to create competitive rates (*Ratcliffe v North Yorkshire CC*);
- woman accepts less (*Clay Cross (Quarry Services) v Fletcher*).

The effects of Europe
Based on A141 – men and women shall receive equal pay for equal work – directly effective provision (*Defrenne v SABENA*).

Broader definition of pay e.g. includes:
- occupational pension schemes (*Barber v Guardian Royal Exchange Assurance Co. Ltd*);
- concessionary travel (*Garland v BREL*).

Difference in pay can be justified by an 'objective justification' (*Bilka-Kaufhaus GMBH v Karen Weber von Herz*).
- corresponds with the genuine needs of business; and
- is proportionate with securing the objective; and
- is necessary for that need.

Can claim under EC law if wider than national law.

6.1 EQUAL PAY

6.1.1 History and Background

1. Equal Pay Act 1970, Equal Pay (Amendment) Regulation 1983, and Sex Discrimination Acts 1975 and 1986, aimed at removing unjustified discrimination against women.
2. Equal pay not a UK but a European concept.
3. By A141 (ex A119): men and women should receive equal pay for equal work – amplified in Directive 75/117.
4. Having both EC and UK law causes some difficulties:
   - supremacy and direct effect of EU law;
   - broader approach of EU law;
   - purposive interpretation used in EU law;
   - ECJ rulings become precedent in UK;
   - EU definition of 'pay' much more generous than UK.

6.1.2 The Equal Pay Act and the Equality Clause

1. By s1(1):
   (a) if any term in a woman's contract is less favourable than in a man's, it is deemed as no less favourable;
   (b) if the woman's contract does not contain a beneficial term in a man's her contract is deemed to contain it.
2. Comparison must be with a person of the opposite sex, in the same or associated employment, engaged in like work, work rated equivalent, or work of equal value.
3. Cannot receive more pay if work of more value (*Murphy v An Bord Telecom Eireann* (1988) and *Waddington v Leicester Council for Voluntary Services* (1977)).

6.1.3 Male Comparitors in the Same Employment

1. Comparitor may be at same establishment or if not must be employed on same terms and conditions; the applicant and comparitor must be typical; and no personal considerations

e.g. red circling and no geographical e.g. London weighting (*Leverton v Clwyd C.C.* (1989)).

2. No claim originally against a 'hypothetical comparitor' HL in (*Macarthy's Ltd v Smith* (1979)) but ECJ accepted comparison with man who previously did the job.

3. Now Employment Appeal Tribunal has accepted a comparison with a man succeeding a woman in the employment (*Diocese of Hallam Trustees v Connaughten* (1996)).

4. Associated employer under A141, it can apply to private and public sector (*Scullard v Knowles* (1996)):
   - and even where there is no associated employer but there is sufficient connection (*South Ayrshire Council v Morton* (2001));
   - but only if difference in pay derives from same source (*Lawrence v Regent Office Care Ltd* (2003)).

5. Claim is not defeated when a token male placed in same job as woman (*Pickstone v Freemans plc* (1988)).

6.1.4 The classes of claim under the 1970 Act

1. Equal pay for 'like work' – under s1(4):
   - defined as work of the same or broadly similar nature (*Sorbie v Trust House Forte Hotels Ltd* (1977));
   - should view broadly (*Capper Pass v Lawton* (1977));
   - and it is the actual work done by each that counts (*Shields v E. Coombes (Holdings) Ltd* (1978));
   - if there is no actual comparitor, tribunal must create a hypothetical one by reference to all actual circumstances (*Shamoon v Chief Constable of the RUC* (2003)).

2. Equal pay for 'work rated as equivalent' – under s1(5).
   - Following voluntary job evaluation scheme by employer – findings must be implemented (*Arnold v Beecham Group Ltd* (1982)).
   - Job evaluation study must be objective analysis (*Bromley v H & J Quick Ltd* (1988)).

3. Equal pay for 'work of equal value' – s2 (1)(c):
   - inserted by Reg. 2 Equal Pay (Amendment) Regulations 1983;

- after UK failure to implement Directive 75/117 & A226 infringement proceedings (*Commission v UK 61/81*);
- appropriate where no man on like work and no voluntary employer's job evaluation study;
- long-winded procedure even after 1996 changes;
- preliminary stage assesses if scheme justified;
- may be denied for 'no reasonable chance of success';
- ACAS expert appointed at discretion of tribunal;
- successful claim is based on study and grading (*Hayward v Camel Laird Shipbuilders Ltd* (1988)).

4. Under the Equal Pay (Questions and Replies) Order 2003 woman uses standard questionnaire to help in decision on issuing claim.

6.1.5 Avoiding equal pay claims under EPA

1. Woman loses claim if employer can show inequality is due to a 'genuine material factor' which is not sex – s1(3).
2. Application varies according to head applied under:
   - in like work and work-rated equivalent, employer MUST prove GMF is reason for variation in pay;
   - in equal value need only show it may be a defence.
3. Genuine material factors have included:
   - geographical location (*NAAFI v Varley* (1977));
   - different responsibilities (*Capper Pass v Allan* (1980));
   - different work done (*Baker v Rochdale HA* (1994));
   - inconvenience (*Calder v Rowntree Mackintosh Ltd* (1993));
   - productivity (*Jenkins v Kingsgate Clothing* (1981));
   - economic necessity (*Rainey v Greater Glasgow Health Board* (1987));
   - red circling (*Methven v Cow Industrial Ltd* (1980)).
4. But certain differences have failed:
   - woman prepared to take lower pay (*Clay Cross (Quarry Services) v Fletcher* (1979));
   - reducing wages for tendering at competitive rates (*Ratcliffe v North Yorkshire County Council* (1995));

- maintaining red circling without reason (*Benveniste v Southampton University* (1989)).

6.1.6 The effects of European law

1. A141 is directly effective (*Defrenne v Sabena* (1976)).
2. Pay more generously defined '… ordinary basic or minimum wage or salary and any other consideration whether in cash or in kind which the worker receives, directly or indirectly, in respect of his employment …'.
3. So pay has included:
   - sick pay (*Rinner-Kuhn v FWW Spezial Gebaudereingung* (1989));
   - concessionary travel (*Garland v BREL* (1982));
   - paid training leave (*Arbeiterwehlifahrt der Stadt Berlin v Botel* (1992));
   - pension schemes supplementing the state's (*Bilka-Kaufhaus GMBH v Karen Weber von Herz* (1984));
   - occupational pension schemes linked to state retirement age (*Barber v Guardian Royal Exchange Assurance Co. Ltd* (1990));
   - unequal retirement ages (*Marshall v Southampton AHA* (1986));
   - redundancy payments (*R v Sec of State for Employment ex p EOC* 1994));
   - and possibly compensation for unfair dismissal (*Mediguard Services Ltd v Thame* (1994)).
4. By Equal Pay (Amendment) Regulations 2003 any award can be for six years from date of commencement of proceedings.
5. But no limit in EC law (*Levez v T H Jennings Ltd* (1999)).
6. So two year limit was declared incompatible with EC law on issue of pension rights for part-timers in (*Preston v Wolverhampton NHS Trust* (2001)).
7. Inequality in part-time work acceptable if 'objectively justifiable' (*Jenkins v Kingsgate Clothing* (1980)).
8. Objective justification is unequal treatment which:
   - corresponds with the genuine needs of business; and
   - is proportionate with securing the objective; and
   - is necessary for that need (*Bilka-Kaufhaus*).

9. Can include employee with different qualifications doing same work (*Angestelltenbetriebstrat der Wiener Gebietskrankenkasse v Wiener Gebietskrankenkasse* (1999)).
10. Can also apply in devising a job evaluation study:
    - scheme as a whole must not be discriminatory;
    - criteria applied must be objectively justified:
        (i) in being appropriate to the task;
        (ii) in corresponding to real needs of business (*Rummler v Dato Druck GMBH* (1985)).
11. Differential pay can be justified in relation to piece-work rates where there is different output, but different time rates must be based on objective justification (*Brunnhofer v Bank der Osterreichischen Postsparkasse AG* (2001)).
12. Coexistence of EC law and EPA is confusing but:
    - EC impliedly overrules any inconsistent national law;
    - If UK law sufficiently wide for claim it should be used;
    - EC law does create in certain cases 'free standing rights' so should be used if wider than national law.

6.2 SEX DISCRIMINATION

6.2.1 Aims of the Sex Discrimination Act 1976

1. SDA 1975 as amended by 1986 SDA and EA 1989 seeks to prevent discrimination on grounds of sex in education; housing; provision of goods, facilities and services and employment.
2. Includes employment under contract of service, apprenticeship or personally to execute any work.
3. It is equally applicable to men.
4. And it applies to married people also s3(1) (a).
5. It is lawful to discriminate against single people (*Sun Alliance & London Insurance Co. v Dudman* (1978)).
6. Act does not permit positive discrimination – in keeping with EC law (*Kalanke v Freie Hansestadt Bremen* (1996)) – but positive action to encourage equality possible if not amounting to preferential treatment (*EFTA Surveillance Authority v Kingdom of Norway* (2003)).

Character of the Sex Discrimination Act

Applies to men and married people (s3) but not single.

Test of what is discrimination is objective not subjective (*James v Eastleigh BC*).

Three types:

- Direct – s1(1)(a) – treats a person less favourably on grounds of his/her sex e.g. failure to give equal access to employment (*Greig v Community Industry*).
- Indirect – s1(1)(b) – applies provisions which mean less of one sex can comply, without justification, and is to complainant's detriment e.g. age restrictions on graduate entry (*Price v Civil Service Commission*), (*Jones v Manchester University*).
- Victimisation – by s4 – discriminates against a person bringing complaint or proceedings under Act or giving evidence in someone else's.

Discrimination in employment

On recruitment and selection – s6(1) unlawful to discriminate in:

- arrangements for selection procedure e.g. interview (*Brennan v Dewhurst*);
- terms employment offered;
- or by deliberately refusing employment (*Batisha v Say*).

During employment – s6(2)(a) unlawful to discriminate in access to transfer, training, promotion or other benefit e.g.:

- pension scheme (*Worrington & Humphries v Lloyds Bank*);
- transfer from part-time to full-time (*Wallace v S E Education & Library Board*);

Or by s6(2)(b) to cause person any other detriment e.g.:

- differential dress codes (*Smith v Safeway plc*);
- sexual harassment (*Porcelli v Strathclyde Regional Council*).

Discriminatory dismissal also unlawful – s6(2)(b):

- no one-year qualifying period for unfair dismissal;
- often involves dismissal on pregnancy (*Webb v EMO AirCargo*).

SEX DISCRIMINATION

Transsexuals and gays

Dismissal purely for transsexualism is discriminatory (*Chessington World of Adventures Ltd v Reed*).

- Comes from ECJ in *P v S and Cornwall County Council* and Sex Discrimination (Gender Reassignment) Regulations 1999.
- But not if for other reason (*Ashton v Chief Constable of West Mercia Constabulary*).
- Discrimination for gay relationship was possible (*Grant v South West Trains*).
- Dismissal was also upheld (*R v Ministry of Defence ex parte Smith*).
- Now is unlawful under 2003 Regulations.

Lawful discrimination

Genuine Occupational Qualifications in s7:

- physical authenticity, e.g. acting;
- preserve decency e.g. close physical contact (*Etam plc v Rowan*);
- entails living in and unfair to expect employer to duplicate provision;
- job in hospital, prison, or other establishing requiring special care and character of establishment requires one sex (*Secretary of State for Scotland v Henley*);
- job involves personal or welfare services requiring one sex;
- job is one involving married couples;
- or working in another country where laws or customs are different (*O'Connor v Kontiki Travel*).

7. Test for whether something is discriminatory or not is objective not subjective (*James v Eastleigh BC* (1990)).

6.2.2 The different characters of discrimination

1. Direct Discrimination under s1(1) (a) is where:
   - on grounds of sex (or marital status) person is treated less favourably than a person of opposite sex (or a single person);
   - so may involve failure to give access to equality of opportunity (*Greig v Community Industry* (1979));
   - or different rules for men and women (*Schmidt v Austick Bookshops* (1978));
   - unless justified (*Smith v Safeways* (1995));
   - no discrimination where rules apply equally to men and women except where there is pregnancy (*Brown v Rentokil Ltd* (1998));
   - it can be discrimination to insist on work being done by one sex (*Jeremiah v M.O.D* (1979));
   - unless the de minimis rule applies (*Peake v Automotive Products* (1978)).

2. Indirect Discrimination under s1 (2) (b) as amended by Sex Discrimination (Indirect Discrimination and Burden of Proof) Regulations 2001 is where there is:
   - application of a provision or requirement applying equally to a person of opposite sex, or single person;
     (i) which is such that it would be to the detriment of a considerably larger proportion of one sex than the other;
     (ii) and it cannot be shown to be justifiable irrespective of sex of person applied to;
     (iii) and it is to the complainant's detriment.
   - change in wording of regulations from 'condition' to 'provision' means woman no longer needs to show that she has to comply with a condition merely that a provision is to her detriment – so decisions like *Price v Civil Service Commission* (1978) and *Turner v Labour Party* (1987) no longer apply;

- what is justified must be measured objectively (*Hurley v Mustoe* (1981));
- and its possible justification weighed against its discriminatory effect (*Allonby v Accrington & Rossendale College* (2001));
- a pool for comparison must be established (*Jones v University of Manchester* (1993));
- it must be determined what proportion can apply (*Kidd v D.R.G. (UK) Ltd* (1985));
- new wording should be more effective in eliminating indirect discrimination – see *Chief Constable of Bedfordshire Constabulary v Graham* (2002).

3. Victimisation under s4 (i):
- unlawful to discriminate because a person has:
    (i) bought proceedings under Acts, or;
    (ii) given evidence or information in proceedings;
    (iii) done anything to discriminator/other person;
    (iv) made allegations of contravention of Act.
- so limited to events during employment (*Waters v Metropolitan Police Commissioner* (1950));
- principle followed in race discrimination for acts after employment (*Post Office v Adekeye* (1997));
- but not possible in sex discrimination since out of line with EU law (*Coote v Granada Hospitality Ltd* (1999)).

6.2.3 Discrimination in selection and recruitment of staff

1. In employment is first and potentially most damaging area.
2. Direct is refusal to employ woman (*Grieg v Community Industries* (1979)).
3. Indirect is imposing a condition more difficult for women to comply with (*Price v Civil Service Commission* (1978)).
4. Three ways discrimination is identified are under s6 (i):
- in arrangements made for selection procedure i.e.
    (i) interview process (*Brennan v Dewhurst Ltd* (1984));
    (ii) though may be possible to ask questions not put to another sex (*Saunders v Richmond on Thames LBC* (1978)).

- in terms on which employment is offered;
- refusing or deliberately omitting to offer employment (*Batisha v Say* (1977) and (*Munro v Allied Suppliers* (1977)).
  - (i) may be discrimination even if no appointment;
  - (ii) fact women have been employed before may defeat claim (*Steere v Morris Bros*).

5. S38 makes discriminatory job advertisements unlawful
   - although it may be objectively justified by a GOQ;
   - only EOC can bring such action.

6.2.4 Discrimination during employment

1. By s6(2) (a) unlawful to discriminate 'in the way a person offers access to opportunities for promotion, transfer or training, or to any other benefits, facilities or services, or refusing or deliberately omitting to afford access to them'.

2. Covers occupational pension schemes (*Worringham & Humphries v Lloyds Bank* (1982)).
   - And transfer from part-time work to full-time work (*Wallace v S E Education & Library Board* (1980)).

3. Must be a disadvantage (*Jeremiah v Ministry of Defence* (1979)).
   - So no claim if too trivial (*Peake v Automotive Products Ltd* (1977)).

4. By s6 (2)(b) unlawful to discriminate by dismissing person or subjecting him/her to any other detriment.

5. Dress code is one such detriment:
   - clear discrimination when rule only applies to one sex (*Smith v Safeway Plc* (1995));
   - but it is possible to have different uniforms (*Burrett v West Birmingham Health Authority* (1994));
   - rules may take into account different conventions (*Schmidt v Austick Bookshops* (1978)).

6. The other major area in s6 (2)(b) is sexual harassment:
   - no definition in domestic legislation – but uses European Commission Codes of Practice 'unwanted conduct of a sexual nature, or other conduct based on sex affecting the dignity of women and men at work';

- includes any unpleasant treatment based on sex (*Porcelli v Strathclyde Regional Council* (1986));
- 'unwanted' can be unwelcome and offensive (*Insitu Cleaning Co. Ltd v Heads* (1995));
- but not 'less favourable' if suffered by man also (*Balgobin v Tower Hamlets LBC* (1987), contrast with *Driskel v Peninsula Business Services* (2000));
- some offensive material is seen as neutral (*Stewart v Cleveland Guest (Engineering) Ltd* (1994));
- must show detriment– though should be construed broadly (*Burton and Rhule v De Vere Hotels* (1996));
- employer can disprove detriment if woman unlikely to be upset (*Wileman v Minilec Engineering Ltd* (1988));
- and evidence of this is admissible (*Snowball v Garden Merchant Ltd* (1987));
- and sexual history can affect woman's claim;
- but more objective view should be taken;
- following recent so-called 'borderline harassment' EAT has produced framework for tribunals to deal with such cases (*Reed; Bull v Stedman* (1999));
- a tribunal cannot hear a complaint of harassment that was only made after the employment was terminated (*Rhys-Harper v Relaxion Group plc* (2001)).

6.2.5 Discrimination on termination

1. By s6 (2) (b) it is unlawful to discriminate by dismissing.
2. Advantageous over normal unfair dismissal claim since:
   - one year qualifying period does not apply;
   - claim can include damages for hurt feelings;
   - no upper limit on compensation;
   - automatically unfair if for pregnancy.
3. May occur in selection for redundancy (*Gubala v Crompton Parkinson* (1977)).
4. Or by non-renewal of fixed-term contracts as part of a redundancy (*Whiffen v Milham Ford Girl's School* (2001)).

5. Or based on sexist assumptions as to the role of women in the family (*Skyrail Oceanic Ltd v Co. Leman* (1981)).

6. But the common area is pregnancy – unlawful under Directive 92/85 and now under ERA 1996 s98:

- originally discounted in UK on argument men cannot become pregnant so no less favourable treatment (like with like approach) (*Webb v EMO Cargo (UK) Ltd* (1992));
- but EU approach different (automatic approach) (*Dekker v Stitchting Vormings Cetrum Voor* and *Jong Wolwassenen (VJV Centrum) Plus* (1991)) compare with (*Handels-OG Kontorfunktionaernes I Danmark v Dansk Handel & Service* (1997));
- some attempts to justify dismissal in radical circumstances (*O'Neill v Governors of St Thomas Moore School & Bedfordshire C.C* (1996)).

7. Discriminatory dismissal not excused on grounds contract is tainted with illegality unless claim arises from the illegal conduct (*Hall v Woolston Hall Leisure Ltd* (2000)).

6.2.6 Lawful sexual discrimination

1. S7 creates means to discriminate lawfully where justified.

2. Called Genuine Occupational Qualification (GOQ) includes:

- authenticity of physiology, e.g. acting, modelling;
- to preserve decency or privacy because:
  - (i) job involves physical contact which could be objectionable, compare *Etam plc v Rowan* (1989) and *Wylie v Dee & Co. Ltd* (1978) with (*Timex Corporation v Hodgson* (1982);
  - (ii) sanitary arrangements;
  - (iii) job involves contact in state of undress (*Sisley v Britannia Security Systems Ltd* (1983));
  - (iv) or living or working in private home and job requires one sex because of degree of social or physical contact.
- location entails living in and unfair to expect employer to duplicate provision;

- job done in hospital, prison, or other establishment requiring special care and with regard to character of establishment one sex is required (*Secretary of State for Scotland v Henley* (1983));
- job involves personal or welfare services requiring one sex to be effectively carried out e.g. Youth Leader in a boys club;
- job is one involving married couples;
- or working in another country where laws or customs are different (*O'Conner v Kontiki Travel*).

3. S3 Employment Act 1989 amends s51 SDA 75, exempting statutory discrimination e.g. night shift, mining no longer prohibited, but s3 retains areas protecting women on pregnancy or specific Health and Safety grounds.

6.2.7 Discrimination against transsexuals and gays

1. Dismissal purely for transsexualism is discriminatory (*Chessington World of Adventures Ltd v Reed* (1997)).
2. Principle originated in ECJ as breach of Directive 76/207 (*P v S and Cornwall County Council* (1996)).
3. Now such discrimination is unlawful under the Sex Discrimination (Gender Reassignment) Regulations 1999.
4. But dismissal is not discriminatory if for another reason (*Ashton v Chief Constable of West Mercia Constabulary* (2000)).
5. Sex Discrimination Act originally could not apply to gays (*Smith v Gardner Merchant* (1996)) but see CA in 1998.
6. Dismissals for homosexuality were upheld (*R v Ministry of Defence ex parte Smith* (1996)) and discrimination on ground of sexual orientation was held lawful (*Grant v South West Trains Ltd* (1998)).
7. Although ECHR has declared this contrary to Article 8 – the right to respect for private life (*Smith & Grady v UK*).
8. Human Rights Act 1998 now incorporates this right – but Act applies to public bodies not private employers.
9. Now such discrimination is unlawful under Employment Equality (Sexual Orientation) Regulations 2003 implementing EU Directive 2003/78 – and see *A v Chief Constable of West Yorkshire Police and Another* (2004) – illegal

discrimination to deny employment to a male to female transsexual on grounds that she would not be able to complete searches under PACE rules.

6.3 RACE DISCRIMINATION

6.3.1 The history and purpose of the Race Relations Act

1. Basic proposition – direct discrimination on grounds of colour, race, ethnic or national origins introduced in Race Relations Act 1965.
2. Supplemented to include 'indirect' in RRA 1968.
3. Phrased in same terms as SDA in RRA 76 and included 'nationality'.
4. 'On racial grounds' subject to argument over time:
   - so 'national origins' originally held as race rather than citizenship (*Ealing B.C. v R.R. Board* (1972));
   - and what is an ethnic group has been questioned (*Mandla v Dowell Lee* (1983));
   - religion is not within the Act (*Crown Suppliers (PSA) v Dawkins* (1991));
   - but Jews (*Seide v Gillette Industries* (1980)) have been held as a racial group; as have gypsies (*CRE v Dutton* (1989));
   - language is not essential to define race (*Gwynedd CC v Jones* (1986)).
5. Original legislation has now been amended in Race Relations (Amendment) Act 2000 and Race Relations Act 1976 (Amendment) Regulations 2003 to comply with EU Directive 2000/43.

6.3.2 Classifications of discrimination

1. Direct is under s1(i)(a) – on racial grounds a person treats someone less favourably than (s)he would treat someone else (*Pel Ltd v Modgill* (1980)):

Classifications of discrimination

Discrimination is unlawful on grounds of colour, race, ethnic or national origins, or nationality.

Direct discrimination under RRA s1(1) (a) is where someone is treated less favourably than another person would be on any of the above grounds (*Pel Ltd v Modgill*).

● So wider than SDA and can be because of another person's race (*Showboat Entertainment Centre Ltd v Owens*).

Indirect discrimination (now defined by 2003 Amendment Regulations) (but not covering colour or nationality):

● applies provision, criteria, practice equally to all racial, ethnic or national origins; but
● puts person at particular disadvantage; and
● not proportionate means of achieving legitimate aim.

Victimisation occurs when person treated less favourably because has:

● brought proceedings under the Act; or
● given evidence in proceedings or done anything under the Act (*TNT Express Worldwide Ltd v Brown*); or
● made any allegations of unlawful discrimination.

RACIAL DISCRIMINATION

Lawful discrimination

Fewer than in SDA:

● authenticity of physiology e.g. modelling;
● preserve ambience of restaurants;
● the welfare provision (*Tottenham Green Under Fives Centre v Marshall*).

Exemptions also apply to:

● private households;
● rules in relation to immigration;
● certain posts within the Civil Service e.g. defence;
● nationality qualifications set for sporting teams.

Discrimination and employment

Before employment can include:

● deciding who is offered job;
● terms of offer of employment;
● refusal to employ or deliberately failing to employ (*Johnson v Timber Tailors*).

During employment it can include:

● terms of employment;
● in way access to promotion; training, transfer, or other benefit, facilities, or services is afforded, or by refusing or omitting to afford such access;
● dismissing person or causing them to suffer any other detriment.

Dismissal can also include discrimination causing constructive dismissal (*Darby Specialist Fabrication Ltd v Burton*).

Detriment includes racial harassment (*Jones v Tower Boot Co. Ltd*).

- so wider than SDA – can cover another person's race (*Showboat Entertainment Centre Ltd v Owens* (1984)) and (*Wilson v TB Steelworks*);
- fact discrimination is for worthy purpose is no excuse (*R v CRE ex p Westminster C.C.* (1984)).

2. Indirect is under s1(i)(b) – it occurs where:
  - a person applies a requirement or condition:
    - (i) such that proportion of one racial group that can comply significantly smaller than another;
    - (ii) and it cannot be justified;
    - (iii) and the complainant suffers a detriment.
  - so requirement must have had to be complied with (*Meer v London Borough of Tower Hamlets* (1988));
  - but no discrimination if requirement justified (*Panesaar v Nestlé Co. Ltd* (1980));
  - 2003 Regulations have added new definition for racial, ethnic, national origins (but not colour or nationality):
    - (i) applies provision, criterion or practice equally to people of all racial, ethnic, national origins; but
    - (ii) put that person at particular disadvantage; and
    - (iii) not a proportionate means of achieving a legitimate aim.

3. Victimisation is under s2 where:
  - person treated less favourably because (s)he has:
    - (i) brought proceedings under Act;
    - (ii) given evidence in proceedings;
    - (iii) done anything under the Act in relation to discrimination (*TNT Express Worldwide Ltd v Brown* (2000));
    - (iv) made allegations of unlawful discrimination.
  - irrelevant to a claim whether there is conscious motivation by the employer. It is enough that the discriminator treated the claimant less favourably because of his/her knowledge of an act coming within the section (*Swiggs and Others v Nagarajan (Nagarajan v London Regional Transport)* (1999));
  - refusal of a reference for a person who has alleged discrimination is victimisation (*Chief Constable of West Yorkshire v Khan* (2000)).

6.3.3 Discrimination and employment under s4

1. Prior to employment unlawful to discriminate on race:
   - in way of determining who is offered employment;
   - in terms on which employment is offered;
   - by refusing/deliberately omitting to offer employment (*Johnson v Timber Tailors (Midlands) Ltd* (1978)).
2. Discriminatory adverts not covered by s4 brought by CRE under s29 (*Cardiff Women's Aid v Hartup* (1994)).
3. During employment unlawful to discriminate on race:
   - in terms of employment which is offered;
   - in way access to promotion, training, transfer, or other benefit, facilities, or services is afforded, or by refusing or omitting to afford such access;
   - in dismissal or subjecting person to any other detriment.
4. Dismissal also includes a constructive dismissal where the employer effectively repudiates the contract by racially discriminating (*Derby Specialist Fabrication Ltd v Burton* (2001)).
5. Detriment means putting person under a disadvantage:
   - So a racial insult by itself is not a disadvantage (*De Souza v AA* (1986));
   - but applying dissimilar conditions is (*B.L. Cars Ltd v Brown* (1983));
   - and as with sex, racial harassment can be a detriment for which the employer will be equally liable (*Jones v Tower Boot Co. Ltd* (1997));
   - harassment now under s3A – violates person's dignity or creates intimidating, hostile, degrading, humiliating or offensive treatment.
6. Post-termination discrimination now unlawful where sufficient connection to employment (*Rhys-Harper v Relaxion Group* (2001)) and now under new s27a inserted by 2003 Regulations.
7. Sex and race discrimination require comparative approach – sometimes conduct is so race/sex specific as to be discriminatory *per se* – but only rarely (*Sidhu v Aerospace Composite Technology Ltd* (2000)).

6.3.4 Lawful discrimination on racial grounds under s5

1. There are less GOQs in RRA than in SDA but including:
   - authenticity in entertainment and for modelling;
   - to preserve ambience of places selling food and drink;
   - in provision of personal or welfare services to a particular racial group, where most effective by member of same racial group – compare *Tottenham Green Under Fives Centre v Marshall* (1991) and *Lambeth London Borough v CRE* (1990).
2. Further possible exceptions include:
   - private households;
   - rules in relation to immigration;
   - certain posts within the Civil Service e.g. defence;
   - nationality qualifications set for sporting teams.

6.4 DISABILITY DISCRIMINATION

6.4.1 Origins

1. Rights first in Disabled Persons (Employment) Act 1944:
   - affected employers with 20 plus employees only;
   - involved voluntary registration as disabled;
   - imposed quotas – 3% of workforce to be disabled;
   - reserved certain occupations for disabled workers.
2. Ineffective so repealed in Disability Discrimination Act 1995 – passed only after much political ill will and 14 failed Private Member's Bills – problems with Act include:
   - only introduced gradually in stages;
   - no provision for indirect discrimination;
   - justifications possible for discrimination;
   - National Disability Council lacks powers of EOC/CRE;
   - no real provision for people with progressive illnesses – covered only once illness affects them, which may encourage employer to discriminate before then.

Definition of disability
Physical or mental impairment having substantial long-term effect on ability to carry out normal day-to-day activities.

Definition of discrimination
- treating disabled less favourable than able bodies (*British Sugar v Kirker*) – without justification (*Baynton v Saurus General Engineers*);
- or failing to honour s6 duties – without justification.

DISABILITY DISCRIMINATION

Unlawful discrimination
Before employment s4:
- arrangements for deciding selection;
- terms offered;
- refusing to offer employment (*Kenny v Hampshire Constabulary*).

During employment:
- terms of employment;
- opportunities for promotion, training, transfer, or other benefits;
- dismissal or causing to suffer any other detriment (*Goodwin v The Patent Office*).

Bringing claims
- Must be an employee (*Sheehan v Post Office Counters Ltd*).
- Claims is to ET.

S6 duties
- Take steps to remove arrangements that may treat disabled worker less favourably.
- But only need do what is reasonably practicable.

6.4.2 Definition of disability

1. Defined in s1(1) – 'physical or mental impairment which has a substantial long-term effect on ability to carry out normal day-to-day activities'.
2. Impairment must have lasted 12 months or be reasonably expected to last that long or for life.
3. Mental impairment must arise from clinical recognised illness (*Goodwin v The Patent Office* (1998)).
4. Even if impairment ceases it may still count if might recur.
5. Impairment affects normal activities if it affects: mobility, manual dexterity, co-ordination, continence, ability to lift or carry, speech, hearing, eyesight, memory, ability to concentrate, learn or understand, perception of dangers.

6.4.3 Unlawful discrimination

1. Identified in s4 – employer must not discriminate:
   - in arrangements for determining selection;
   - in terms offered;
   - refusing to offer or failing to offer employment (*Kenny v Hampshire Constabulary* (1998)).
2. During employment must not discriminate:
   - in terms of employment;
   - in opportunities for promotion, training, transfer or other benefit or by refusing any such opportunity;
   - by dismissal or causing to suffer any other detriment (*Goodwin v The Patent Office* (1998) and *Clark v Novacold Ltd* (1998));
   - under s3B by harassing the disabled person (same definition as for race);
   - or under s55 by victimising the disabled person who has brought an action under the Act.

6.4.4 Meaning of discrimination

Now under s3A – an employer discriminates if (s)he:
- treats disabled worker less favourably than (s)he would an able bodied one (*British Sugar v Kirker* (1998));
- and cannot show any justification (*Baynton v Saurus General Engineers* (1999));
- discriminates on basis of general assumptions about the disability; or
- fails to comply with a s6 duty without justification.

6.4.5 S6 duties

1. To take reasonable steps to remove arrangements that may treat disabled employee less favourably.
2. May include conditions for promotion, training, transfer and also physical features of the premises.

3. May require adapting premises, assigning to different workplaces, modifying equipment, providing specialist facilities e.g. interpreter, allowing absence related to the disability (*Kenny v Hampshire Constabulary* (1998)).
4. But is set against practicality, cost, and extent to which arrangements are able to remove the disadvantage.

6.4.6 Claiming and remedies

1. Must be employee (*Sheehan v Post Office Counters Ltd* (1999)).
2. By s8 – as usual complaint is to ET.
3. ET can make declaration, award compensation (including injured feelings), make recommendation (with power to increase compensation if employer fails to comply).
4. Reporting restrictions can be issued by Secretary of State if embarrassing for petitioner, or Lord Chancellor for EAT.

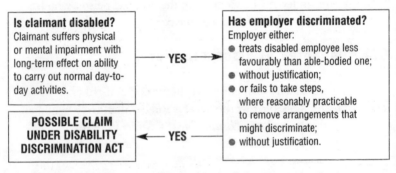

Flow chart illustrating liability under Disability Discrimination Act

6.5 DISCRIMINATION ON TRADE UNION GROUNDS

6.5.1 General

1. Rights protected include membership, non-membership, and trade union activities.
2. Found in TULR[C]A '92, TURERA '93 and ERA '96.

Access to employment

Unlawful to refuse employment by TULR[C]A 92 if person not member of TU, or will not join or leave TU, or will not accept deductions for TU. Rule does not cover self-employed or:

- members of armed forces and serving police officers;
- share fishermen;
- employees ordinarily working outside GB;
- seamen registered on non-British ships;
- people ordinarily resident outside of the UK;
- exemptions granted by Secretary of State on grounds of national security e.g. GCHQ.

Can discriminate for past activities (*Birmingham City Council v Beyer*). Membership and activities can overlap – compare *Harrison v Kent County Council* with *Associated British Ports v Palmer*. Remedies are in ss 139–142 e.g. declaration, compensation.

Action short of dismissal

TULR[C]A s146 gives right not to be disciplined to:

- deter TU membership; or compel membership; or
- deter taking part in TU activities at appropriate time.

Appropriate time for TU activities is:

- own time (*Robb v Leon Motor Services*);
- in working hours with consent (*Brennan and Ging v Ellward (Lancs) Ltd*).

Must show employer's action was for reasons above (*Associated Newspapers v Wilson*). Purpose is not to be confused with effect (*Gallacher v Department of Transport*). Any penalty imposed on employee may count, not just punishment (*Carlson v The Post Office*). Burden on employer to show other reason. Complaint to tribunal should be within three months: may award compensation – based on actual loss (*Cheall v Vauxhall Motors Ltd*).

DISCRIMINATION ON TRADE UNION GROUNDS

Time off

Time off for TU duties:

- by TULR[C]A s168 employer must allow official of recognised TU time off during working hours to: carry out duties connected with office; take part in training.

Time off for TU activities:

- by s170 legitimate if for e.g. conferences, but not industrial action.

Dismissal

Dismissal for official strike only unfair if other strikers not dismissed or re-engaged within three months – s238(I)(b).
Not entitled to redundancy even if dismissed for industrial action (*Baxter v Limb Group*).
Employer can re-engage any striker after three months – but loses protection of s238 if dismisses:

- before a strike (*Midland Plastics v Till*);
- after strike (*Heath v Longman (Meat Salesmen) Ltd*).

Rules also apply to other industrial action e.g. working without enthusiasm (*Thomson v Eaton Ltd.*) and work to rule (*Secretary of State for Employment v ASLEF*).
No right to claim unfair dismissal in unofficial action.

6.5.2 Access to employment

1. By TULR[C]A s137 unlawful to refuse employment if:
   - person is not a member of trade union; or
   - will not accept requirement to become or cease to be a union member, or accept deductions if not in TU.
2. Refusal to employ can take many forms.
3. Rule does not apply to self-employed; nor does s137 cover following employees:
   - members of armed forces and serving police officers;
   - share fishermen;
   - employees ordinarily working outside GB;
   - seamen registered on non-British ships;
   - people ordinarily resident outside of the UK;
   - national security exemptions e.g. GCHQ.
4. It is possible to discriminate for past union activities (*Birmingham City District Council v Beyer* (1978)).
5. Membership and activities can overlap a question of fact in each case: compare *Harrison v Kent CC* (1995) with *Associated British Ports v Palmer* (1995).
6. Advertisements linked with membership, non-membership, are presumed to be discriminatory.
7. S138 extends same provisions to Employment Agencies.
8. Remedies are found in ss139–142:
   - complaint should be made within three months;
   - tribunal must make declaration, may award compensation, or recommend remedial action.

6.5.3 Action by employer short of dismissal

1. TULR[C]A s146 gives right not to be disciplined to:
   - deter TU membership; or compel membership; or
   - deter taking part in TU activities at appropriate time.
2. Appropriate time for TU activities is:
   - in own time (*Robb v Leon Motor Services* (1978));
   - during working hours with express or implied consent (*Brennan and Ging v Ellward (Lancs) Ltd* (1976)).

3. Must show employer's action was for reasons above (*Associated Newspapers v Wilson* (1993)):
- purpose of discriminating is not to be confused with effect (*Gallacher v Department of Transport* (1994));
- and any penalty imposed on employee may count, not just punishment (*Carlson v The Post Office* (1981)).

4. Burden of proof is on employer to show other reason.

5. Complaint to tribunal should be within three months:
- may award compensation – based on actual loss (*Cheall v Vauxhall Motors Ltd* (1979));
- by s12 Employment Relations Act 1999 cannot discipline employee for exercising right to be accompanied at hearing or accompanying another.

6.5.4 Time off for Trade Union duties

1. By TULR[C]A s168 employer must allow official of recognised TU time off during working hours to:
- carry out any duties connected with his/her office;
- take part in training in industrial relations.

2. Amount of time off is what is reasonable in ACAS Codes.

3. Refusing time off can be challenged (*Blower v CEGB*).

6.5.5 Time off work for Trade Union activities

1. By s170 this is for legitimate activities e.g. conferences.

2. But not industrial action – which is never legitimate.

6.5.6 Trade Union related dismissals

1. Dismissal for membership, non-membership or union activities automatically unfair – no qualifying period s154.

2. Union activities must take place in own time or work time with consent (*Britool Ltd v Roberts* (1993)).

3. Legitimate Trade Union activities include:
- collecting subscriptions (*Zucker v Astrid Jewels Ltd* (1978));

- seeking advice from Union representatives on appropriate matters (*Stokes & Roberts v Wheeler Green Ltd* (1979));
- posting notices (*Post Office v UPW & Crouch* (1974));
- negotiating for union recognition (*Taylor v Butler Machine Tool Co. Ltd* (1976)).

4. Holding meetings in work time with corresponding loss of production is less likely to be legitimate (*Marley Tile Co. Ltd v Shaw* (1980)).

5. By s12 Employment Relations Act 1999, dismissal for exercising right to be accompanied or accompany another worker at disciplinary hearing in s10 is unfair.

6.5.7 Dismissal for taking part in industrial action

1. Dismissal after lock-out only unfair if other employees not dismissed, or re-engaged within three months- s238(1)(a).

2. Dismissal in relation to official strike only unfair if other strikers not dismissed or dismissed but re-engaged within three months – s238(I)(b).

3. Employee dismissed for striking not entitled to redundancy even if leads to redundancy (*Baxter v Limb Group of Companies* (1994)).

4. Employer can re-engage any striker after three months – but loses protection of s238 if dismisses:
   - before any strike (*Midland Plastics v Till* (1983)); or
   - after (*Heath v Longman (Meat Salesmen) Ltd* (1973)).

5. Rules also apply to other industrial action e.g. go-slows, sit-ins, working without enthusiasm (*Thompson v Eaton Ltd* (1976)), and work to rule (*Secretary of State for Employment v ASLEF* (1972)).

6. No right to claim unfair dismissal for unofficial action:
   - involves members on unauthorised action, or non-members where two other strikers are on official action;
   - but not unofficial action if none are TU members.

6.5.8 Dismissal for industrial pressure on employer

1. By s10 ERA dismissals where employer under threat of industrial action are unfair.
2. ET by s107 ERA cannot take account of this reason, so unfair if no other reason (*Hazells Offset v Luckett* (1977)).

6.6 DISCRIMINATION AND RELIGION AND BELIEF

1. EU A141 is base for introducing Directives based on equal treatment and equal opportunities.
2. A141 still limited to sexual equality but separate clause A13 allows Commission to take appropriate action to combat discrimination based on 'sex, racial or ethnic origin, religion or belief, disability, age, or sexual orientation'.
3. Provisions of Directive 2003/78 implemented in Employment Equality (Religion or Belief) Regulations 2003.
4. Religion or belief defined as any religion, religious belief or other philosophical belief:
   - so obvious for e.g. Catholics, Muslims, Jews;
   - but less so for e.g. Druids, Satanists, animal rights activists;
   - and does not cover political belief.
5. Mirrors other discrimination law and covers harassment and victimisation.
   - but exceptions where religion is a 'genuine and determining occupational requirement';
   - or where is 'determining' but not 'decisive' requirement and is proportionate.

Procedure
- By s76 SDA complain within three months
- Must be within three months of continuing act ceasing (*Calder v James Findlay*) or three months of act with continuing consequences itself (*Sougrin v Haringey HA*)
- Burden of proof on employer to show is not discrimination
- Can argue vicarious liability (*Strathclyde Regional Council v Porcelli*)
- EOC and CRE can begin proceedings and devote resources, instigate formal investigation
- Only EOC and CRE can bring action against discriminatory advertising.

Remedies
Three possible orders:
- declaration of infringement of employee's rights;
- award of compensation;
- recommendation to end discrimination within specified time.

Damages on tort scale – includes hurt feelings (*Snowball v Gardner Merchant Ltd*).
Following *Marshall (No. 2)* and Equal Pay Remedies Regulations 1993 – now no upper limit – so some big awards (*MOD v Cannock*).
Judicial Review possible (*R v Sec of State for Employment ex parte EOC*).

CLAIMING

6.7 PURSUING DISCRIMINATION CLAIMS

6.7.1 Procedure for claiming

1. Anyone can bring a complaint within three months of act complained of (s76 SDA s54 RRA). But see *Preston v Wolverhampton Healthcare NHS Trust* (1998).
2. Must distinguish between act of continuing discrimination and act with continuing discriminatory consequences:
   - in first, claim must be within three months of act ceasing (*Calder v James Findlay Corporation Ltd* (1989));
   - In second claim must be within three months of act itself (*Sougrin v Haringey Health Authority* (1993)).
3. Burden of proof is now on employer to show there is no discrimination:

- Sex Discrimination (Indirect Discrimination and Burden of Proof) Regulations 2001 (inserting new s63A into SDA);
- 12 guiding principles identified in *Barton v Investec Henderson Crosthwaite Securities Ltd* (2003);
- racial discrimination now under s54A RRA – can infer from primary facts.

4. Can argue vicarious liability (s41 SDA, s32RRA) (*Strathclyde Regional Council v Porcelli* (1986)):
   - providing act complained of is within course of employment (*Irving v Post Office* (1987));
   - and employer can escape liability for worst harassment (*Tower Boat Co. Ltd v Jones* (1995)).

5. EOC and CRE can start proceedings for an individual (s73 SDA s58RRA):
   - devote resources to assist claim, instigate formal investigations (s75 SDA s66 RRA);
   - only EOC and CRE can bring actions on discriminatory advertising or instructions or pressure to discriminate (s72 SDA s63RRA);
   - both can issue non-discrimination notices, make recommendations, obtain County Court injunctions.

6. Discrimination claim can survive death of claimant (*Lewisham & Guys Mental Health NHS Trust v Andrews (Deceased)* (2000)).

6.7.2 Remedies

1. If complaint successful, tribunal has three possible orders:
   - declaration of infringement of employee's rights;
   - award of compensation against the employer;
   - recommendation to end discrimination within specified time (non-compliance can result in extra compensation).

2. Damages are on tort scale – so damages for injury to feelings possible – but only if some injury has been sustained (*Snowball v Gardner Merchant Ltd* (1987)).

3. Traditionally awards were subject to two major limitations:
   - calculated up to unfair dismissal maximum;
   - no compensation for indirect if no intention shown.

4. Overcome first by EC law (*Marshall (No 2)* (1994)):
- upper limit now removed by Equal Pay Remedies) Regulations 1993, and Race Relations (Remedies) Act 1994;
- some massive awards (*MOD v Cannock* (1995));
- new Regulations in SI 1996 no. 438 allow compensation for unintentional indirect discrimination;
- so UK standards are now possibly in line with EC.

5. Judicial Review is also possible e.g. *R v Sec. of State for Employment ex parte EOC* (1995).

CHAPTER 7

HEALTH AND SAFETY LAW

The non-delegable duty in *Wilson v Clyde Coal Co. v English*:
Must provide competent staff for duties undertaken (*General Cleaning Contractors v Christmas*):
● So must ensure good behaviour (*Hudson v Ridge Manufacturing*).
Must provide safe plant and equipment:
● and properly maintain it (*Smith v Baker*);
● but now Employer's Liability (Defective Equipment) Act 1969 applies.
Must take reasonable steps to provide safe premises (*Latimer v AEC*).
● May extend to other premises (*Wilson v Tyneside Cleaning Co.*).
Must provide safe system of work:
● must create and implement safe system;
● and ensure system carried out (*Bux v Slough Metals*);
● must meet dangers (*General Cleaning Contractors v Christmas*);
● cannot rely on unsafe system just because common practice (*re: Herald of Free Enterprise*).
Now applies also to psychiatric health and well-being (*Walker v Northumberland CC*), and on providing references (*Spring v Guardian Assurance Co.*).

COMMON LAW HEALTH AND SAFETY

Defences
Volenti (consent) – limited use since *Smith v Baker*.
● possible if agreement free from pressure (*ICI v Shatwell*);
● and claimant sole cause of injury (*Ginty v Belmont Building Supplies Ltd*);
● but not for breach of statute.
Contributory negligence – possible defence to any duty:
● damages may be reduced when worker contributed to own injury (*Jones v Livox Quarries Ltd*);
● 100% reduction possible (*Jayes v IMI (Kynoch) Ltd*).

Character of duty
● non-delegable (*Wilson & Clyde Coal Co. v English*);
● only need do what is reasonable (*Latimer v AEC*);
● extends to reasonable and incidental activities (*Davidson v Handley Page Ltd*);
● does not extend to employees properly (*Deyong v Shenburn*);
● trade practices can only be relied upon if reasonable (*Cavanagh v Ulster Weaving Co*);
● should consider possible extent of injury (*Paris v Stephney BC*);
● may consider practicality of any precautions (*Charlton v Forrest Printing Ink Co*);
● must prevent only reasonably foreseeable accidents (*Doughty v Turner Manufacturing*).

7.1 COMMON LAW PROVISIONS

7.1.1 Origins

1. Industrial safety law developed after Industrial Revolution.
2. Employment traditionally seen as contract, based on freedom of contract – so no remedies in tort.
3. Three major nineteenth-century barriers to protection of employees:
   - *Volenti* – worker said to consent to risks of work.
   - Contributory negligence – a total defence at that time.
   - Common employment – no liability on employer where a 'fellow servant' caused the injury.
4. Most nineteenth-century safety law was in statute.
5. Harshness of common law defences eventually limited.
   - (*Smith v Baker* (1891)) *volenti* only available if claimant genuinely free to choose to take the risk.
   - Law Reform (Contributory Negligence) Act 1945 – not complete defence but reduces damages.
   - Common employment no defence to breach of statutory duty in *Groves v Lord Wimbourne* (1898), abolished in Law Reform (Personal Injury) Act 1948.
6. Three further important developments:
   - *Wilson & Clyde Coal Co. v English* (1938) created concept of personal, non-delegable duty to provide:
     (i) safe, competent working colleagues;
     (ii) safe plant and equipment ;
     (iii) safe premises;
     (iv) a safe system of work.
   - Employers Liability (Defective Equipment) Act 1969 – employer liable for defective equipment without fault.
   - Workmen's Compensation Act 1897 formed insurance principle, guaranteed to all employers by Employment Liability (Compulsory Insurance) Act 1969.
7. Industrial safety now means employer is liable for:
   - Breach of a statutory duty e.g. Health and Safety at Work Act 1974 and numerous statutory instruments.

- Vicarious liability – for the tortuous acts of employees in the course of their employment.
- Personal non-delegable common law duty of care.

7.1.2 The duty to provide competent staff

1. Employees must be competent for duties they undertake (*General Cleaning Contractors Ltd v Christmas* (1953)).
2. Employer must ensure good behaviour of staff, and dismiss if necessary – compare *Hudson v Ridge Manufacturing Co.* (1957) with *O'Reilly v National Rail and Tramway Appliances* (1966).
3. Useful if employee's act is not in course of employment.

7.1.3 The duty to provide safe plant and equipment

1. Employer must provide proper equipment and properly maintain it (*Smith v Baker* (1891)).
2. But may avoid liability if employee fails to use equipment properly (*Parkinson v Lyle Shipping Co. Ltd* (1964)).
3. Less important since Employers' Liability (Defective Equipment) Act 1969.
4. Act itself has been subject to interpretation of equipment:
   - includes hull of ship (HL reversing CA) (*Coltman v Bibby Tankers* (1988));
   - and kerbstone (*Knowles v Liverpool CC* (1993)).

7.1.4 The duty to provide a safe place of work

1. Employer must take such steps as are reasonable to make premises safe (*Latimer v AEC* (1953)).
2. Duty may extend to premises other than the employer's (*Wilson v Tyneside Cleaning Co.* (1958)).
3. Liability also possible under Occupiers Liability Act 1957.
4. Though much of duty now falls within the 'six pack'.

7.1.5 The duty to provide a safe system of work

1. Duty has two aspects:
   - creation of a safe system;
   - implementation of the system.
2. Question of fact if system necessary or safety obvious.
3. Cannot rely on unsafe practice merely because it is common practice (*Re Herald of Free Enterprise* (1989)).
4. Duty is to provide effective system to meet the danger (*General Cleaning Contracters v Christmas* (1953)).
5. And to ensure it is operated (*Bux v Slough Metals* (1974)).
6. And to ensure system does not cause undue stress (*Walker v Northumberland County Council* (1994)).
7. So must warn of dangers (*Pape v Cumbria CC* (1992)).
8. Duty may extend to method of using equipment (*Mughal v Renters* (1993)).
9. And to training employees to use equipment (*Mountenay (Hazzard) & Others v Bernard Matthews* (1993)).
10. And to rotating work properly (*Mitchell v AtCo.* (1995)).
11. But employees are expected to be aware of risks associated with their skills (*Roles v Nathan* (1963)).

7.1.6 Recent developments

1. New duty to protect psychiatric well-being of employee (*Johnstone v Bloomsbury Health Authority* (1991)).
2. So a new field is developing on stress-related illnesses and psychiatric damage caused at work:
   - began as a duty to protect the psychiatric health and well-being of the employee (*Petch v Commissioners of Customs and Excise* (1993));
   - employee entitled to treat psychiatric injury caused by negligent work practice in same way as physical injury (*Walker v Northumberland CC* (1995));
   - so can be liability for stress caused by abuse and physical danger in workplace (*Ingram v Worcestershire County Council* (1999));

- and by bullying and harassment in the workplace (*Ratcliffe v Dyfed County Council* (1998));
- and by redeployment and changing job roles (*Lancaster v Birmingham City Council* (1998));
- but duty limited to when reasonable employer would foresee stress suffered likely to be of such degree as to cause a recognised psychiatric disorder and that (s)he should do something about it (*Sutherland v Hatton* (2004) – restrictive guidelines by House of Lords mean stress claims are less easy to bring).

3. While an employer has no duty to provide a reference another new duty is not to negligently prepare references for employees (*Spring v Guardian Assurance Co.* (1994)).

7.1.7 The character of the duty

1. Entirely personal and non-delegable (*Wilson & Clyde Coal Co. v English* (1938)).

2. But only to do what is reasonable – not guarantee safety (*Latimer v AEC* (1935)).

3. Duty extends to reasonable and incidental activities (*Davidson v Handley Page Ltd* (1945)).

4. Duty does not necessarily extend to employees properly (*Deyong v Shenburn* (1946)).

5. Trade practices can only be relied upon if reasonable (*Cavanagh v Ulster Weaving Co.* (1960)).

6. Duty extends to considering the possible extent of injury (*Paris v Stephney BC* (1951)).

7. Employer may take into account the practicality of any precautions (*Charlton v Forrest Printing Ink Co.* (1978)).

8. Employer should prevent reasonably foreseeable accidents, compare *Doughty v Turner Manufacturing* (1964) with *Bradford v Robinson Rentals* (1967).

7.1.8 Defences

1. *Volenti* (consent) – limited use since *Smith v Baker* (1891):
   - but possible in genuine agreement free from pressure – compare *ICI v Shatwell* (1965) with *Baker v T E Hopkins* (1959);
   - and if claimant sole cause of injury (*Ginty v Belmont Building Supplies Ltd* (1959));
   - by policy unavailable for breach of statutory duty.
2. Contributory negligence – possible defence to any duty:
   - Employees generally given more leeway (*Caswell v Powell Duffryn Collieries* (1940));
   - to protect them from their own carelessness (*General Cleaning Contractors v Christmas* (1953));
   - damages may be reduced when worker contributed to own injury (*Jones v Livox Quarries Ltd* (1952));
   - or death (*Davies v Swan Motor Co. Ltd* (1949));
   - 100% reduction possible (*Jayes v IMI (Kynoch) Ltd* (1985)).

7.2 STATUTORY AND EU PROTECTIONS

7.2.1 General

1. Volume of accidents demonstrates need for effective regulation.
2. Common law originally hostile so early developments statutory.
3. Defects in law as it developed in statute were obvious:
   - was found in many Acts – so was cumbersome;
   - was complex and often overlapped;
   - was based on premises rather than people;
   - many workers fell outside of cover.
4. Robens Committee in 1970 was set up to review whole area:
   - acknowledged above defects and also the number of bodies and ministries involved;

- suggested three levels of control: broad based legislation; regulations and codes of practice; and voluntary codes.
5. EU law also crucial e.g. 'six pack', working time directive.

7.2.2 Health and Safety at Work Act 1974 – general

1. Covers people rather than premises.
2. Brought seven million more workers within cover.
3. Has included trainees on government schemes since Health and Safety (Training for Employment) Regs. 1990.
4. Based on criminal sanctions – but also looks for co-operation with employers through voluntary codes.
5. By s2(1) duties of employer are '… to ensure so far as is practicable health, safety and welfare of employees', including:
   - to provide and maintain safe plant and systems;
   - to ensure absence of risks in handling, storing, transport, use of articles and substances;
   - to inform, instruct, train and supervise where necessary;
   - to maintain premises, access, exits etc.;
   - to provide a safe working environment without risks.
6. Welfare not defined but includes e.g. sanitary arrangements.
7. By s2(3) must produce written safety policy statement:
   - based on individual needs of workplace;
   - minimum contents include individual responsibilities and procedures, emergency procedures identified;
   - can seek guidance from HSC.
8. Major innovation in s2(4), (6), (7) is duty to have safety reps:
   - and duty is to consult with safety reps;
   - safety reps responsibilities include e.g investigating hazards and causes of injuries, taking complaints to employer, inspections, liaising with appropriate bodies etc.
9. Further specific duties of employer include:
   - by s44 ERA 1996 not to cause an employee detriment for involvement in legitimate HASAW activity;
   - or by s100 ERA 1996 not to dismiss on HASAW reasons – which is an automatically unfair dismissal;

Health and Safety at Work Act 1974 – general

Covers people rather than premises.

By s2(1) employer's duty is so far as is practicable to ensure HASAW and welfare of employees including:

- provide and maintain safe plant and systems, premises, exits;
- remove risks in handling, storing, transport of articles/substances;
- inform, instruct, train, supervise;
- provide safe working environment.

S2(3) requires HASAW policy statement.

S2(4) requires safety representatives.

S4 must not cause employee detriment.

S100 – dismissal for asserting any HASAW right is automatically unfair.

S3 extends employer's HASAW duties to people other than employees.

S6 duty on manufacturers, designers, importers, suppliers to ensure articles and substances are free from risks and tested.

S7 also places duty on employee to take care of self and others.

Regulations and enforcement of HASAW 1974

Three types of regulations possible:

- those laying down standards applying to all employment;
- those controlling specific hazards in particular industries;
- those controlling specific hazards which cross industries

Act set up two separate bodies:

- Health and Safety Commission – to administrate the law;
- Health and Safety Executive – to enforce the law.

Inspectors have powers to:

- enter premises, investigate, make examinations; take photographs, samples; make recordings; seize documents; take custody and control of hazardous substances;
- issue improvement Notices and Prohibition Notices.

STATUTORY AND EU HEALTH AND SAFETY

Regulations from EU directives

Major Regulation introduced to give effect to EU directives:

Management of HASAW Regulations 1999:

- risk assessment, health surveillance, safety officers, emergency procedures, training.

Workplace (HASAW) Regulations 1992:

- efficient maintenance and repair, clear air, proper lifting, sanitation etc.

Provision and Use of Work Regulations 1998:

- suitable and efficient work equipment, proper controls on machines.

Personal Protection Equipment at Work Regulations 1992:

- all PPEs must be in good repair and conform to EU standards.

Manual Handling Operations Regulations 1992:

- reduce manual handling, reduce risks.

Health and Safety (Display Screen) Equipment Regulations 1992:

- work stations, eye tests, change of activities.

Working Time Regulations

Regulations apply to:

- Employees: those under a contract to provide personal services but not as a business or profession e.g. voluntary workers; agency staff.
- But not: self-employed; trainee doctors; armed forces; share fishermen and other workers at sea.

Basic provisions:

- 48 hour week;
- eight hour night work limit;
- 11 hour minimum daily rest period;
- 24 hour minimum weekly rest period;
- 20 minutes after six hours minimum break period;
- four weeks paid holiday;
- health checks.

- by s3 HASAW duty also extends to ensure health and safety of other people;
- by s4 HASAW to ensure against risks in all access, exits plant and premises;
- and by s5 HASAW to avoid emissions of noxious or offensive substances into the atmosphere;
- by s6 HASAW there is a duty on manufacturers, designers, importers and suppliers of articles or substances:
  (i) to ensure they are free from risks;
  (ii) to test such articles/substances and to provide necessary information etc.

10. Duties of employees and others:
    - by s7 employee has duty to take care of self and others;
    - and to co-operate fully with employer on HASAW issues;
    - by s8 all persons owe duty not to intentionally or recklessly interfere with or misuse anything provided for HASAW.

7.2.3 Regulations authorised by s15 and Schedule 3 of the Act

1. Act replaced old system of individual statutes – so gives power to introduce regulations by statutory instrument and also Codes of Practice to advance HASAW.
2. Three types of regulations are possible :
   - those laying down standards applying to all employment;
   - those controlling specific hazards in particular industries;
   - those controlling specific hazards which cross industries.
3. Usually introduced in statutory instrument by Secretary of State after Health and Safety Commission (HSC) recommendation.
4. Regulations can repeal or amend existing provisions; grant authority to specific bodies; identify parties subject to criminal sanctions; grant exemptions and also under Schedule 3 insist activities are only carried out under licence.

7.2.4 Enforcement of the Act and related Regulations

1. Act set up two separate bodies:
   - Health and Safety Commission – to administrate the law.
   - Health and Safety Executive – to enforce the law.
2. Enforcement is by Inspectors with wide powers:
   - enter premises (with support of police if necessary);
   - investigate, carry out examinations, take photographs, samples, make recordings, seize documents;
   - take custody and control of hazardous substances/situations;
   - require relevant parties to answer questions;
   - use any other power necessary to carry out their duties.
3. By s21 Inspectors may issue Improvement Notices:
   - where any HASAW provisions have been contravened;
   - notice cites provision breached, indicates improvement required, and period within which improvement must occur.
4. By s22 Inspector can issue Prohibition Notice:
   - where breach of provision involves risk of personal injury;
   - notice prohibits that activity until risk is removed.
5. Employers may appeal against either type of notice.
6. S25 gives power to take whatever action is required in a situation of imminent danger.
7. By s42 courts can order employer to take steps to eliminate risks as well as imposing fines.

7.2.5 EU Law and HASAW

1. EU is a major provider of HASAW law through A118A (inserted by Single European Act) with power to issue Directives in furtherance of HASAW (by qualified majority voting).
2. Many already adopted and implemented in UK as Statutory Instruments – but many more exist in draft form.
3. Major group of Regulations from Directives is the 'six pack' introduced in 1993 as amended – significant feature of Directives is requirement for pro-active steps e.g. risk assessments.

4. Management of Health & Safety at Work Regulations 1999:
- basic requirement of risk assessment (particularly women of child bearing age and young people);
- provide health surveillance for employees;
- appointment of safety officers;
- must establish emergency procedures;
- must provide necessary training;
- employees legal duty to comply with all procedures.

5. Workplace (Health and Safety and Welfare) Regulations 1992:
- applies to all workplaces after January 1996;
- requires efficient maintenance, repair, and cleaning;
- and pure air, reasonable temperature, adequate lighting;
- and provision of seats when work can be done seated;
- controls construction of doors, ladders etc.;
- provision of adequate sanitary arrangements;
- provision for changing clothes where necessary.

6. Provision and Use of Work Regulations 1998:
- work equipment must be suitable, efficiently maintained, kept in good repair and conform to EC requirements;
- employees must be given appropriate information;
- effective steps must be taken to prevent access to dangerous parts of machinery;
- proper controls on entry to machines, stopping controls etc. and immediate isolation.

7. Personal Protection Equipment at Work Regulations 1992:
- PPE covers anything to be worn or held to protect employees from HASAW risks;
- must conform to EU standards or is unsuitable;
- all such equipment must be compatible with any other used;
- and should be kept in good repair;
- employer must ensure it is used properly.

8. Manual Handling Operations Regulations 1992:
- must reduce manual handling which carries risks;
- employer must produce an assessment of operations;
- if manual handling unavoidable then employer must do everything possible to minimise risk.

9. Health and Safety (Display Screen) Equipment Regulations 1992:
- must analyse workstations to assess HASAW risks;

- and there is a duty to reduce such risks;
- and provide planned periodic breaks or change of activity;
- and provide eyesight testing;
- and provide adequate information and training.

7.2.6 The Working Time Regulations

1. Only introduced after change of government, and previous government's failure to resist EU enforcement procedures.
2. Regulations lack clarity, are full of exemptions covering certain types of work and certain classes of employee.
3. But employee required to opt out, and has right to opt back in – and employer must keep records.
4. Basic provisions:
   - 48 hour week averaged out over 17 week period;
   - limits on night work – 8 hours in 24;
   - minimum daily rest period – 11 hours, 12 if young worker;
   - minimum weekly rest period – 24 hours, 48 if young worker;
   - minimum rest break periods – 20 minutes after 6 hours (or 30 for young workers);
   - adequate rest breaks where monotony of work puts worker's health at risk (though no definition of 'adequate');
   - minimum paid holiday entitlement of four weeks;
   - free health checks for night workers.
5. Regulations apply to:
   - employees working under a contract of employment;
   - those under a contract to provide personal services but not as a business or profession e.g. voluntary workers;
   - agency staff.
6. Regulations do not apply to:
   - self-employed;
   - trainee doctors; the armed forces; share fishermen and other workers at sea;
   - those with autonomous decision-making powers;
   - where there is a signed derogation agreement.
7. Basic remedy of employee might be claim of constructive dismissal – criminal as well as civil sanctions apply e.g. fines.

CHAPTER 8

TUPE Transfers

8.1 General background

To whom Regulations apply

By Reg 2(1) applies to 'any individual who works for another person, whether under contract of service, apprenticeship, other.' Nature of undertaking now in *Cheesman v R Brewer Contracts Ltd*.

- Stable economic entity – organised grouping of assets and persons, enabling exercise of economic activity.
- Sufficiently structured and autonomous.
- Assets can be minimal and activity be based mainly on manpower.
- Organised group of wage earners permanently assigned to a task can be an economic entity.
- Activity alone is not an entity – depends on many factors.

Nature of a transfer

Relevant transfer can be sale, or other disposition or by operation of law **but must be change in identity of employer** (*Young v Daniel Thwaites*), key question is whether business has retained its identity (*Dines v Initial Health Care Services*). ECJ at one point ignored whether assets transferred (*Schmidt v Spar und Leihkasse*). But standard test is that in *Ayse Suzen v Zehnake Gebaudereinigung GmbH* – must be transfer of economic entity not just activity. Principles now summarised in *Cheesman v R Brewer Contracts Ltd*:

- Entity must retain identity.
- If labour intensive must retain major part of numbers and skills.
- Must consider all factors.
- If entity functions without assets – then transfer of assets not vital to TUPE rights.
- Absence of contract not conclusive.
- Fact work continues uninterrupted is common feature of TUPE.

TUPE

Effect of transfer

By Reg 5(1) transfer does not terminate employment. Transferee **'steps into shoes' of transferor** (*Morris Angel & Son Ltd v Hollande*). Reg. 5(2) on transfer transferor's rights, powers, duties and liabilities in employment contract transfer to transferee e.g. tort claims (*Martin v Lancashire County Council*). So unfair dismissal claim possible (*Litster v Forth Dry Dock & Engineering*). Any attempt to alter conditions of employment may be void (*Wilson v St Helens Borough Council*), (*Meade and Baxendale v British Fuels Ltd*).

Dismissals

By Reg 8(1) if dismissal before or after transfer is principally for reason of transfer then is automatically unfair. Unless dismissal is for an economic, technical, or organisational reason (ETO reason). CA has expressed conflicting views on methods of testing if TUPE dismissal is unfair (*Warner v Adnet* and *Whitehouse v Chas A Blatchford & Sons*).

Consultation

By Reg. 10 before transfer must inform employees of:

- fact, date of, and reasons for transfer;
- legal, social and economic implications of transfer;
- likely effect of transfer on employees.

By Collective Redundancies and Transfer of Undertakings (Protection of Employment) (Amendment) Regulations 1999 should be with recognised Trade Union.

1. Original common law position was that contract ceased on transfer of business – so no obligation on transferee.
2. Transfer of Undertakings (Protection of Employment) Regulations 1981 passed to implement Acquired Rights Directive 77/187 – since amended in TU(PE)(Amendment) Regulations 1995.
3. Aims of Directive were:
   - ensuring consultation with employees affected by a transfer;
   - ensuring transfer of contracts of employment;
   - ensuring maintenance of collective agreements for one year;
   - transfer itself not to be reason for any dismissals;
   - dramatic changes in working conditions after transfer to count as dismissal.
4. TUPE rights and obligations should be interpreted purposively – because they represent EC law (*Litster v Forth Dry Dock & Engineering Co. Ltd.* (1990)).
5. For Regulations to apply tribunal must be certain of two facts:
   i) there was a relevant and sufficiently identifiable economic entity;
   ii) there was a relevant transfer (*Whitewater Leisure Management Ltd v Barnes* (2000)).

8.2 TO WHOM REGULATIONS APPLY

1. Applies to employees – 'any individual who works for another person, whether under a contract of service or apprenticeship or otherwise' (Reg. 2(1)).
2. They apply to a transfer of an undertaking – includes any trade or business, but also e.g. charities.
3. And to a part of the undertaking (if self-contained).
4. Can be problematic if employee works for holding company and its subsidiary (*Sunley Turriff Holdings Ltd v Thomson* (1995)).
5. Or where employee performs functions for both transferred and retained parts (*Botzen v RDM* (1985) and *Duncan Web Offset (Maidstone) Ltd v Cooper* (1995)).

6. NHS and other government departments now have guidelines on application of TUPE to contracting out cases. Effect is TUPE should always apply unless exceptional, genuine reasons not do so. Should also be appropriate arrangements for pensions, redundancy, severance.

7. EAT has recently summarised relevant principles to determine what is an undertaking for TUPE purposes in *Cheesman v R Brewer Contracts Ltd* (2001):
   - Must be a stable economic entity not limited to performing one works contract, and an organised grouping of assets and persons, enabling the exercise of an economic activity.
   - Must be sufficiently structured and autonomous.
   - It is possible for assets to be minimal and activity to be based mainly on manpower.
   - Organised group of wage earners permanently assigned to a task can be an economic entity.
   - Activity alone is not an entity – depends on workforce, management, organisation, operating methods etc.

8.3 THE NATURE OF A TRANSFER FOR TUPE PURPOSES

1. A relevant transfer can be a sale, or any other disposition or by operation of law.

2. But there must be a change in the identity of the employer (*Young v Daniel Thwaites & Co. Ltd* (1977));
   - and the absence of a contractual link between transferor and transferee will not stop TUPE applying if there is an indirect link (*Temco Service Industries SA v Imzilyen* (2002).

3. It is not a TUPE transfer if merely assets are transferred.

4. A transfer by operation of law is where the company is dissolved but continues to operate (*Charlton v Charlton Thermosystems (Romsey) Ltd* (1995)).

5. ECJ has applied principle to services (*Rask v ISS* (1993)).

6. Key question on transfer is whether business has retained its identity (*Dines v Initial Health Care Services* (1995)).

7. ECJ at one point seemed to extend Directive to virtually all business transfers regardless of whether or not there was a transfer of tangible assets (*Schmidt v Spar und Leihkasse der Fruheren Amter Bordesholm, Kiel und Cronshagen* (1994)).

8. But have returned to position where transfer must be of an economic 'entity' not simply an economic 'activity' (*Ayse Suzen v Zehnake Gebaudereinigung GmbH Kraankenhausservice* (1997));
   - and there is no reason in principle why the work of a single employee cannot be classed as an economic entity (*Dudley Bower Building Services Ltd v Lowe* (2003)).

9. But in service contracts it is possible for transferee to decide if Directive applies by decision to engage or not (*Betts v Brintel Helicopters Ltd and KLM ERA Helicopters (UK) Ltd* (1997)).

10. Tension and confusion has developed between *Suzen* approach and more purposive approach:
    - CA in *ECM (Vehicle Delivery Services) Ltd v Cox* (1998) suggests that there is no conflict between *Suzen* and *Schmidt*;
    - On occasions *Schmidt* has been followed in preference to *Ayse Suzen* (*Argyll Training Ltd v Sinclair* (2000));
    - *Suzen* followed by ECJ in *Oy Liikenne AB v Liskojarvi* (2002) – staff transferred without assets so identity not retained and no TUPE transfer;
    - CA in *ADI (UK) Ltd v Willer* (2001) followed *Suzen* and *ECM*;
    - CA in *RCO Support Services v UNISON* (2002) said TUPE transfer not precluded because neither assets nor workforce transferred;
    - CA in *P & O Trans European Ltd v Initial Transport Services Ltd* (2003) held that decision should not be based on single factor.

11. EAT summarised principles to determine whether there is a transfer in *Cheesman v R Brewer Contracts Ltd* (2001):
    - The entity must retain its identity – operation is actually continued or resumed.
    - In labour intensive activities the entity can retain its identity after transfer if new employer not only continues

activity but takes over major part of workforce in terms of numbers and skills.

- All factors must be considered – and none should be considered in isolation.
- Factors for consideration include: type of undertaking, whether tangible assets are transferred, value of intangible assets at time of transfer, whether majority of employees taken on by new owner, whether customers transferred, degree of similarity of activities.
- Must take account of type of business.
- If the economic entity is able to function without tangible or intangible assets, maintenance of identity after transfer will not depend on transfer of assets.
- Fact assets do not transfer does not preclude TUPE.
- Maintenance work carried out firstly by a cleaning firm then by owners of premises does not automatically make a TUPE transfer.
- Absence of contract between transferor and transferee may mean there is no relevant transfer but this is not conclusive.
- If no employees are transferred this can be relevant.
- Fact that work continues uninterrupted and unchanged is a common feature of a TUPE transfer.

12. New Acquired Rights Directive (Directive 98/50) has been accepted which mostly follows (*Suzen*). Directive gives greater degree of discretion to the member states than original Directive.

8.4 THE EFFECT OF THE TRANSFER

1. By Reg. 5(1) a relevant transfer does not terminate employee's contract – transferee 'steps into shoes' of transferor (*Morris Angel & Son Ltd v Hollande* (1993)).
2. Employee can refuse to transfer but will lose rights unless:
   - employer failed to consult/inform in advance of transfer;
   - substantial change of conditions amounting to constructive dismissal (*University of Oxford v Humphreys* (2000)) but

must amount to a repudiatory breach going to root of contract (*Rossiter v Pendragon* (2002));

● and if refuses to transfer will lose claim to unfair dismissal (*Katsikas v Konstantinidis* (1993).

3. By Reg. 5(3) provisions apply if employed 'immediately before transfer' (*Apex Leisure Hire v Barratt* (1984)):

● so possible unfair dismissal claim (*Secretary of State for Employment v Spence* (1987), *Litster v Forth Dry Dock & Engineering Co. Ltd* (1990)).

4. By Reg. 5(2) on completion of relevant transfer:

● transferor's rights, powers, duties and liabilities under employment contract transfer to transferee – so e.g. tortious rights against employer are transferred (*Martin v Lancashire County Council* (2000)) as are statutory rights e.g. equal pay, maternity (*Alamo Group (Europe) Ltd v Tucker* (2003);

● this is at least partly mitigated by fact employer's benefits are also transferred to new employer (*Bernadone v Pall Mall Services Group Ltd* (2000));

● anything done in relation to contract prior to transfer is deemed to have been done by transferee (*DJM International Ltd v Nicholas* (1996)).

5. Pension rights do not automatically transfer.

6. Collective agreements between transferor and recognised Trade Unions do transfer.

7. Any attempt to alter conditions of employment may be void (*Wilson v St Helens Borough Council, Meade* (1996) and *Baxendale v British Fuels Ltd* (1997)).

8. Employee and new employer may agree to alteration in relationship but invalid if transfer is reason for alteration – contrast *Martin v South Bank University* (2004) and *Norris v Brown & Root Ealing Technical Services Ltd* (2002).

8.5 DISMISSAL ON TRANSFER

1. Reg. 8(1) allows that: where either before or after relevant transfer an employee of transferor or transferee is dismissed

then dismissal automatically unfair if transfer is principal reason for dismissal.

- But Reg. 8(2) allows that dismissal may be fair if for: an economic, technical or organisational reason (EOT reason) requiring a change of workforce (provided employer acts reasonably).
- Reg. 8(2) is construed narrowly (*Wheeler v Patel & Goulding Group* (1987)).
- So it is not an automatically unfair dismissal if the receiver dismisses staff.

2. Employee's rights in dismissal, even if before transfer, are against transferee not transferor (*Allan v Stirling District Council* (1995)).

3. According to HL appeals in *Wilson v St Helens Borough Council* and *Meade and Baxendale v British Fuels Ltd* (1997), when employee is dismissed for a reason connected to a TUPE transfer, dismissal is effective and it is only secondary obligations arising out of the dismissal that are transferred to transferee.

- Exception is dismissal for an economic, technical or organisational (an EOT) reason – therefore, it is liability in respect of unfair or wrongful dismissal that is transferred (which reversed the reasoning in CA that the dismissal would be a nullity and employee would have rights of continued employment).
- CA has made area more complex by apparently taking conflicting views on means of testing whether TUPE dismissal is unfair. Compare *Warner v Adnet* (1998) with *Whitehouse v Chas A Blatchford & Sons* (1999).

4. It is now also possible for an employee to refuse to transfer under Reg 5 (4A) and thus be able to claim a constructive dismissal (*Humphreys v Oxford University* (2000)):

- despite the traditional effects of Reg 5 (4B) which meant that an employee refusing to transfer was considered not to have been dismissed.

8.6 CONSULTATIONS

1. Reg. 10 requires that an employer consults before any transfer and informs employees of:
   - fact of, date of, and reasons for transfer;
   - legal, social and economic implications of transfer;
   - likely effect of transfer on employees.
2. Consultation was originally through the employee's elected representatives.
3. Information must be given long enough before transfer to allow for a meaningful consultation to occur.
4. Any failure to consult might give rise to action in a tribunal.
5. Under Collective Redundancies and Transfer of Undertakings (Protection of Employment) (Amendment) Regulations 1999, now, if there is a recognised trade union, Regulations provide for primacy of that union over other elected representatives in collective consultation on redundancies and transfers.
6. Now, despite previous authorities to contrary, liability under a protective award for a failure to consult workforce is one of liabilities that transfers to transferee (*Kerry Foods Ltd v Creber* (2000)).
7. Duty to consult clearly also includes position where an employer, despite claim that there is no actual redundancy, takes on all staff but then dismisses them in order to force through major changes in contract (*GMB v Man Truck and Bus UK Ltd* (2000)).
8. Changes from Directive 98/50 are to be implemented:
   - greater protection for public sector employees on outsourcing in protection of occupational pensions, redundancy and severance;
   - definition of economic entity from *Spijkers v Gebroeders Benedik Abbatoir CV* (1986) to be used in outsourcing – organised grouping of resources with objective of pursuing economic activity;
   - transferee to be notified of all outstanding rights and any changes;
   - rights to agree changes on insolvency if for survival of enterprise;
   - union recognition to be preserved.

Continuity of employment
- Employment protections based on continuous service e.g. unfair dismissal one year, redundancy two.
- Continuity begins when contract says not actual start (*General of Salvation Army v Dewberry*).
- Ends on actual termination.
- Some acts do not break continuity and count:
  - illness, injury;
  - temporary cessation;
  - customary absence;
  - pregnancy.
- Some break continuity and do not count:
  - strikes;
  - illegality.

Notice
- Termination should be by notice period in contract.
- Or statutory minimums are:
  - one week if over four weeks' and under two years' service;
  - one week per year to maximum 12 if over two years' service;
  - employee must give one week's minimum.
- Employee entitled to which ever is the greater.
- Contract can end before end of notice period if pay in lieu of notice accepted – or summary dismissal justified.

CONTINUITY, NOTICE AND DISMISSAL

Dismissal
- Dismissal by ss95–6 ERA 1996 is when:
  - employer dismisses employee with or without notice;
  - fixed term expires without renewal;
  - employee legitimately claims constructive dismissal.
- Constructive is when employee leaves and claims no other choice:
  - must be based on breach by employer of term going to root of contract (*Western Excavating v Sharp*);
  - But employee must still show dismissal was unfair.
- Summary is when employer dismisses without notice for misconduct:
  - usually requires gross misconduct;
  - can be gross insubordination (*Wilson v Racher*);
  - or drunkenness (*Hadden v Van den Bergh's Foods*);
  - or dishonesty (*Sinclair v Neighbour*);
  - or acts of violence.

9.1 CONTINUITY, NOTICE AND DISMISSAL

9.1.1 Continuity of employment

1. Most employment protection rights require a period of continuous employment e.g. unfair dismissal – one year, redundancy – two years.
2. Continuity is defined in ss212 – 218 Employment Rights Act 1996, changes to the contract do not generally mean that the contract terminates and a new one begins.
3. Continuity begins when contractual employment rather than actual employment begins (*General of the Salvation Army v Dewberry* (1984)) and ends on termination of the contract.
4. Certain acts will not break continuity and count towards computation of the period:
   - periods of illness or injury;
   - temporary cessation of work;
   - arranged or customary absences;
   - pregnancy.
5. Other acts break continuity of employment but will not count towards computation of the period:
   - strikes;
   - illegality in the contract.

9.1.2 Notice

1. Termination by employer should be by giving notice – the period of notice will be in the contract.
2. There are also statutory minimum notice periods which must be adhered to:
   - Employees between four weeks and two years service are entitled to one week.
   - Employees over two years are entitled to one week for every year of service up to a maximum of 12 weeks.
   - Employees should give a minimum of one week's notice.

3. An employee is entitled to whichever is the greater, and contractual notice under the statutory minimum is void.

4. A contract can terminate before the end of the notice period where the employee accepts pay in lieu of notice, or where summary dismissal is justified.

9.1.3 Dismissal

1. An employee can class himself/herself as dismissed according to ERA ss95-6 if:
- contract terminated by employer with or without notice, but mere warning of possible future dismissal is not dismissal (*Rai v Somerfield Stores Ltd* (2004));
- (s)he is employed on a fixed-term contract which expires without being renewed, if for genuine fixed term – now to be treated no less favourably than permanent employees by Fixed Term Employees (Prevention of Less Favourable Treatment) Regulations 2002;
- employee terminates in circumstances in which (s)he is entitled to claim constructive dismissal.

2. A constructive dismissal is one where the employee resigns his/her position and claims it as an effective dismissal resulting from the conduct of the employer.
- Question for tribunal is what conduct by the employer justifies the employee claiming constructive dismissal.
- Must be conduct representing breach going to root of contract (*Western Excavating v Sharp* (1978)).
- But the fact that there is a constructive dismissal does not necessarily mean that the dismissal is unfair – that must still be proved.
- Generally such conduct is unilateral changes in terms of employment or breach of duties towards employee e.g.failing to protect from harassment.

3. Summary (instant) dismissal occurs where the employer dismisses without notice for disciplinary breach.

4. Only possible where justified by the employee's conduct:
- so usually based only on gross misconduct;

Nature of wrongful dismissal claims
- Common law action arising only if:
  - employed under fixed-term contract;
  - employed under contract stipulating only grounds for dismissal.
- Breach of contract so claim for damages only.
- Can claim in tribunal since Industrial Tribunals Extension of Jurisdiction Order 1994.
- Action useful to three groups only:
  - on fixed term and dismissed within term;
  - highly paid employees e.g. executive directors;
  - excluded from claiming unfair dismissal.

Bringing a claim
- Rule against enforcement usually applies (*De Francesco v Barnum*).
- So only available remedy is damages.
- Exceptions to rule are:
  - negative restraint (*Lumley v Wagner*);
  - dismissal is a nullity e.g. *ultra vires* (*Ridge v Baldwin*);
  - the rule in *Hill v CA Parson & Co. Ltd*.

WRONGFUL DISMISSAL

Damages
Is for remainder of fixed term or notice period.
Exceptions are:
- if fixed term not terminable by notice then remainder of term;
- if greater reward envisaged in contract (*Marbe v George Edwards (Daly's Theatres) Ltd)*;
- if wrongful dismissal puts employee outside unfair dismissal limits.
Employee should try to mitigate loss.

- originally gross insubordination was sufficient (*Wilson v Racher* (1974));
- Acts of dishonesty also justify summary dismissal (*Sinclair v Neighbour* (1967));
- as can acts of drunkenness (*Hadden v Van den Bergh's Foods* (1999));
- or acts of violence.

9.2 WRONGFUL DISMISSAL

9.2.1 The nature of wrongful dismissal claims

1. Traditional common law action arising where either:
   - employee is employed under a fixed-term contract; or
   - employee is employed under a contract that stipulates the only possible grounds for dismissal.
2. So is for breach of contract and concerned only with form of dismissal – actionable as breach of contractual term.
3. In unfair dismissal the merits of the situation are the critical elements in determining the outcome of the case.
4. It is possible to claim both wrongful and unfair dismissal.
5. Wrongful claim is for damages only – reinstatement or re-engagement are not available – nor compensation for mental distress (*Johnson v Unisys Ltd* (2001)).
6. Claim in tribunal possible since Industrial Tribunals Extension of Jurisdiction Order 1994.
7. Ineffective for most employees since their periods of notice are so short that damages would be minimal.
8. So action is important for three specific groups of workers:
   (i) those on fixed-term contracts dismissed within term;
   (ii) highly-paid employees e.g. executive directors where statutory maximum for unfair dismissal means they lose out (fewer since increase to £50,000);
   (iii) employees excluded from unfair dismissal claims.

9.2.2 Bringing an action for wrongful dismissal

1. Courts will not directly or indirectly enforce employment contract (the 'rule against enforcement') as relationship is highly personal (*De Francesco v Barnum* (1890)).
2. S236 Trade Union and Labour Relations (Consolidation) Act 1992 prevents court from issuing such an order.
3. So only available remedy is damages – employee must accept employer's unlawful repudiation of contract and sue for damages (which is inconsistent with contract law).
4. There are exceptions to the rule against enforcement:
   - a negative restraint clause: court will hold employee to a contract in which (s)he has promised not to do certain things (*Lumley v Wagner* (1852));
   - where the dismissal is a nullity: may occur in judicial review for breach of natural justice or a decision *ultra vires* the employer (*Ridge v Baldwin* (1964)) – though applies only if dismissal is a public law issue (*R v East Berkshire Health Authority ex parte Walsh* (1984));
   - the rule in *Hill v CA Parsons & Co. Ltd* (1972): injunction granted because rule against enforcement is one of fact not law so subject to exceptions e.g. damages inadequate remedy – rare but followed in *Hughes v London Borough of Southwark* (1988).

9.2.3 Damages

1. Damages are salary for remainder of fixed term or that which could have been received during the normal period of notice if contract contains break clause.
2. Courts are reluctant to increase this e.g. with damages for injured reputation (*Addis v The Gramophone Co.* (1909)) or for the difficulty of finding a new job (*Boardman v Copeland Borough Council* (2001)).
3. Or for increases that have occurred after the dismissal (*Lavarack v Woods of Colchester Ltd* (1967)).

4. Exceptions to this basic rule include:
- if contract is for fixed term not terminable by notice damages are amount employee would have earned during remainder of term; and may include accrued pension rights (*Silvey v Pendragon plc* (2001));
- if contract envisages greater reward than basic salary damages should reflect this (*Marbe v George Edwards (Daly's Theatres) Ltd* (1928));
- if wrongful dismissal means employee falls outside of unfair dismissal, qualifying period damages should reflect loss of statutory claim.

5. Employee is under a duty to mitigate his/her loss:
- must take reasonable steps to find comparable work;
- but not just any work – though after reasonable time employee may have to be less selective.

6. Award takes into account tax and other contributions employee would have paid – but not taxed unless over £30,000.

7. Benefits paid after dismissal are deductible from award – though contrary has been held for particular reasons e.g. where personal injury involved.

9.3 UNFAIR DISMISSAL

9.3.1 General background

1. Concept first created in Industrial Relations Act 1971.

2. Now found in s94-107 Employment Rights Act 1996.

3. Act distinguishes:
- automatically unfair dismissals – always unfair, and;
- potentially fair dismissals – only fair if carried out fairly.

4. Any action depends on:
- claimant being employed;
- continuity of employment;
- presence of an actual dismissal.

9.3.2 Eligibility

1. By s94 ERA 1996 every employee '… has the right not to be unfairly dismissed'.
2. But certain workers are excluded from the provisions:
   - independent contractors;
   - share fishermen;
   - those reaching normal retirement age in contract of employment, or 65 if none, except if discriminatory;
   - members of the constabulary;
   - those working solely outside of Great Britain regardless of employer's base (*Lawson v Serco Ltd* (2004));
   - agreed exemptions authorised by Secretary of State e.g. in collective agreements with trade unions;
   - those engaged in industrial action, providing all are dismissed and none is taken back within three months.
3. Also ineligible are all those with less than one year's continuous service – unless any of the following applies:
   - dismissal for legitimate trade union activities;
   - dismissal for asserting a statutory right;
   - dismissal for asserting any Health and Safety right;
   - dismissal related to pregnancy or parental leave;
   - discriminatory dismissal;
   - dismissal of a shop worker or betting office worker refusing to work on a Sunday;
   - medical dismissal (qualifying period one month);
   - undertook jury service.

9.3.3 Dismissals classed as automatically unfair

1. By Trade Union and Labour Relations (Consolidation) Act 1992 s152 a dismissal for legitimate trade union activities:
   - membership/non-membership are protectable rights – so cannot be dismissed for either (*Discount Tobacco & Confectionery Ltd v Armitage* (1995));
   - but this would not include unofficial activities (*Dick v Aberdeen Scaffolding Ltd*).

Eligibility

By s94 ERA 96 every employee has right not to be unfairly dismissed except: self-employed, sharefishermen, over retiring age, exemptions agreed by Sec of State, strikers; and less than one year's service, except if: asserting statutory right, legitimate TU activities, asserting HASAW right, pregnancy related, discriminatory, medical, or shop worker refusing Sunday work.

Potentially fair dismissals

Law gives employer right to dismiss if: potentially fair reason and fairly carried out.

Five potentially fair reasons in s98 ERA 96:

Capability and qualifications of employee – can be:

- incompetence justifying dismissal (*Woods v Olympic Aluminium Co*);
- or the employer's health (*McPhee v George Wright*);
- or failing to comply with an essential qualification of the work (*Tayside Regional Council v McIntosh*).

Misconduct of the employee – can be:

- refusal to obey lawful and reasonable instructions (*Hann & Edwards v Crittal Hope*);
- serious breach of discipline (*Parsons v McLoughlin*);
- absenteeism (*International Sports Ltd Thomson*);
- criminal offences if they have a bearing on the work (*Moore v C & A Modes*).

Genuine redundancy – requiring objective criteria/fair selection.

Statutory restriction – business shut down e.g. foot and mouth.

Other substantial reason – catch all category e.g.:

- ETO reason; or non renewal of fixed-term contract; or
- dismissal of one of a couple where the other partner is already dismissed.

UNFAIR DISMISSAL

Bringing claims and remedies

Claim within three months with certain exemptions.

Three types of remedy:
(i) reinstatement – given same job back on same terms;
(ii) re-engagement – taken back for other work on no worse conditions;
(iii) compensation – can have basic award and compensatory award – latter includes e.g. hurt feelings – ceiling of £55,000 except in e.g. discrimination claims (*Marshall (No. 2)*).

ACAS Arbitration scheme also possible now since 2001.

Automatically unfair dismissals

- For legitimate Trade Union activities; or industrial action if unequal treatment; or unfair selection for redundancy on TU grounds.
- On TUPE transfer (*Litster v Forth Dry Dock & Engineering Co*) unless for economic, technical or organisational reason (EOT).
- Any reason connected to pregnancy (*Webb v EMO*).
- Any HASAW related reason.
- 'Whistle blowing' under Public Interest Disclosure Act 98.
- For asserting any statutory right.
- Employer fails to carry out SDDP.

Test if dismissal is fair

Must hold genuine belief, and reasonable grounds justifying dismissal (range of reasonable responses test) (*British Home Stores v Burchill*).

Test in *Iceland Frozen Food v Jones*:

Use words from s98(4) ERA:

- ask if employer acted reasonably;
- tribunal must not substitute own view of right response;
- band of reasonable responses different;
- employers might take different views;
- must decide if dismissal was in reasonable range of responses reasonable employer might take.

Test now approved in *Foley v Post Office*; *Midland Bank v Madden*, despite contrary view in *Hadden v Van den Bergh's Foods*.

2. Dismissals for industrial action where there is unequal treatment – ss237–239 TULR(C)A 1992.

3. Unfair selection for redundancy on trade union grounds – s153 Trade Union Reform & Employment Rights Act 1993

4. Dismissal on a Transfer of Undertakings:
   - if employee dismissed on business changing hands then can be automatically unfair (*Litster v Forth Dry Dock & Engineering Co.* (1989));
   - or employee might claim constructive dismissal for a complete change in working practices;
   - but employer may claim necessary for 'economic, technical or organisational reasons' (*Meikle v McPhail* (1983)).

5. Dismissals for any reason connected to pregnancy ERA s98 (*Stockton-on-Tees BC v Brown* (1988)) or parental leave:
   - supported by EC law (*Webb v EMO Air Cargo* (1994));
   - applies if not allowed to return (*Clayton v Vigers* (1989));
   - by TUR & ERA 1993 s23 there is no qualifying period;
   - employer cannot justify dismissal on pregnancy alone by claiming illegalities in contract make contract void (*Hall v Woolston Hall Leisure Ltd* (2000)).

6. Dismissals for any Health and Safety at Work related reason under s100 ERA – because employee has duties to ensure HASAW as much as the employer.

7. Dismissals for asserting any statutory right.

8. Dismissal for exercising a right under the Public Interest Disclosure Act 1998.

9. Dismissal of a shop or betting office worker who refuses to work on Sunday s101 ERA.

10. Dismissal that fails to apply statutory disciplinary and dismissal procedure (SDDP) ERA s98A.

9.3.4 Potentially fair dismissals

1. Law recognises employer must have the right to dismiss.

2. Two key points apply:
   - certain recognised reasons where employer may need to dismiss – so accepted as potentially fair;

- potentially fair does not make fair in fact – employer still must justify dismissal in law when claim made.

3. So once employee proves that there was a dismissal burden shifts and employer must show:
   - actual reason for dismissal;
   - that reason for dismissal is one Act accepts as potentially fair i.e. a reason which is *prima facie* fair;
   - that it was fair in fact.

4. S98 ERA 1996 gives only five reasons justifying dismissal:
   - capability and qualification;
   - misconduct;
   - a fair selection under a genuine redundancy scheme;
   - a dismissal because of a statutory restriction;
   - any other substantial reason (obviously the one that gives employers most flexibility to dismiss).

5. The capability and qualifications of the employee:
   - capability refers to the skill, aptitude, health or other mental or physical quality of the employee;
   - qualification refers to any academic, technical or professional qualification relevant to the position held.
   Capability then might fall into two categories:
   (i) it might involve incompetence justifying dismissal (*Woods v Olympic Aluminium Co.* (1975));
      (a) but not if employee was properly instructed (*Davison v Kent Meters Ltd* (1975));
      (b) and proper disciplinary procedure should be followed (*Lowndes v Specialist Heavy Engineering Ltd* (1977));
      (c) but the longer an employee's service the more difficult it is to prove (*Hooper v Fedex* (1974));
      (d) in extreme cases summary dismissal may be justified (*Taylor v Alidair* (1978)).
   (ii) it might also concern health of employee if resulting in a continued inability to work (*McPhee v George Wright* (1975)).
      (a) and there is no requirement to create a special job for a sick employee (*Merseyside and North Wales Electricity Board v Taylor* (1975)).

    (b) though employer cannot presume employee is unfit
    to return because of risk of further illness
    (*Converform (Darwen) Ltd v Bell* (1981)).

    (c) qualifications will usually arise as an issue because
    an employee lies about qualifications:

       (i) but may also be an issue when employee is no
       longer able to do work (*Tayside Regional Council
       v McIntosh* (1982)).

6. Misconduct is legitimate reason for dismissal but must follow
own disciplinary procedures or can be unfair:

- so refusal to obey lawful and reasonable instructions
justifies dismissal (*Hann & Edwards v Crittall Hope* (1972));

- and dismissal may be appropriate where disciplinary
standards are infringed sufficiently seriously (*Parsons v
McLoughlin* (1978));

- persistent absenteeism may justify dismissal (*International
Sports Ltd v Thomson* (1980));

- and criminal offences may justify dismissal if they have a
bearing on the work (as criminal records may impact on
whether to employ) (*Moore v C&A Modes* (1981));

- but will not if they do not affect the work (*Norfolk County
Council v Bernard* (1979));

- and dismissal for dishonesty must follow a proper
investigation and be measured against proper legal test for
dishonesty (*John Lewis plc v Coyne* (2001));

- for conduct outside work to justify dismissal it must be
incompatible with the work and potentially damaging (*Pay
v Lancashire Probation Service* (2004) or destroy confidence
in employee (*Whitlow v Alkanet Construction Ltd* (1975)).

7. Genuine redundancies:

- a *prima facie* fair reason for a dismissal;

- but must conform to necessary procedures;

- there must be an objective criteria for selection;

- the person must be fairly selected by the criteria;

- also vital that the employer should consult criteria in
Mugford v Midland Bank plc (1997);

- although ultimately employer should be looking for alternative ways of dealing with problem;
- obviously a subject of many claims;
- discrimination might also be an issue.

8. Dismissal because of a statutory restriction:
   - could arise because business is prevented from operating by statute or other regulation;
   - or because the employer is prevented from operating (*Mathieson v Noble & Son Ltd* (1972)).

9. Other substantial reasons:
   - catch-all category for situations not otherwise covered;
   - possible to claim dismissal is for economic, organisational or technical reasons (EOT reasons);
   - variety of possibilities:
     - (i) dismissal of one of a couple where the other partner is already dismissed;
     - (ii) dismissal of employee misrepresenting facts to procure employment;
     - (iii) non-renewal of fixed-term contracts;
     - (iv) genuine need for reorganisation.

9.3.5 Determining whether dismissal is fair

1. Tribunal can consider numerous factors in determining the fairness of a dismissal:
   - duty to consult employee at all stages;
   - existence/effect of express or implied terms;
   - breaches of mutual trust and confidence;
   - introductions of new rules or procedures;
   - procedural faults;
   - instances of gross misconduct;
   - blanket dismissals;
   - selection criteria in redundancy;
   - breaches of duty of fidelity;
   - internal hearings and appeals procedure;
   - nature of sickness;
   - natural justice.

2. Tribunal will use a statutory test to determine whether the dismissal is fair taking into account:
   - circumstances of case;
   - behaviour of employee;
   - proper use of disciplinary or grievance procedures;
   - consistency of treatment.
3. Employer must act reasonably (*British Home Stores v Burchill* (1978)) – and base decision to dismiss on genuine belief, based on reasonable grounds, following reasonable investigation that there were grounds to justify dismissal (the range of reasonable responses test).
4. Five stage test for tribunal was outlined in detail by Browne – Wilkinson J in *Iceland Frozen Foods v Jones* (1983):
   - begin with words of s98(4) – whether employer acted reasonably, judged by equity and merits of case;
   - must consider whether employer acted reasonably – not whether or not they think the dismissal was fair;
   - tribunal must not substitute its own decision as to what the right course was for the employer to adopt;
   - there is a band of reasonable responses to employee's conduct in which different employers might take different views;
   - must determine whether dismissal was in reasonable range of responses a reasonable employer might take.
5. CA has since suggested that there is nothing intrinsically wrong in the tribunal substituting its own view for that of employer – so ignoring 'range of reasonable responses test' (*Haddon v Van den Bergh's Foods Ltd* (1999)).
6. But in *Midland Bank v Madden* (2000) EAT suggested that no court short of the Court of Appeal can discard the range of reasonable responses test, although accepting that the *Burchill* test might simply go to reason for the dismissal rather than the reasonableness of the dismissal.
7. Joined appeals (*Foley v Post Office*; *Midland Bank v Madden* (2000)) CA have clarified the position:
   - the band of reasonable responses approach to the test of reasonableness in s98(4) remains intact;
   - Browne-Wilkinson's test in *Iceland Frozen Foods* is approved;

- three-part test in *Burchill* is approved;
- so ultimate test is whether, by standard of reasonable employer, employer acted reasonably in treating reason shown for dismissal as a sufficient reason.

9.3.6 Bringing actions and remedies

1. A claim for unfair dismissal must be made to tribunal within three months of effective date of termination of contract:
   - an exception is under s238 and 238A TULR[C]A 1992 – for dismissals following protected industrial action;
   - if out of time tribunal has no jurisdiction to hear case (*Glennie v Independent Magazines Ltd* (1999));
   - by s111(2)(b) ERA 1996 tribunal may hear claims out of time if satisfied it was not reasonably practicable to present claim in time (*Cavaciuti v London Borough of Hammersmith & Fulham* (1991));
   - for internal appeals time runs according to whether on proper construction of contract employee is suspended pending outcome of appeal or not (*Drage v Governors of Greenford High School* (2000)).
2. Where employee is dismissed for wrong reason and this is discovered on appeal, EAT must consider whether dismissal for that reason not the other was reasonable (*Wilson v Post Office* (2000)).
3. There are three available remedies for an unfair dismissal:
   - reinstatement;
   - re-engagement;
   - a compensatory award.
4. In fact the first two would rarely be granted because of difficulty of administering them or breakdown in relations. Test for tribunal is 'practicability' not 'possibility'.
5. Reinstatement:
   - means that the employer must take the employee back in the same job;
   - effect is as if the employee has not been dismissed;
   - so continuity of employment is protected;

- and employee is eligible for back pay, and any improvement in terms (s)he would have received if still in work.
6. Re-engagement:
   - means that the employee must be taken back on by the employer or an associated employer on terms comparable with those (s)he enjoyed when dismissed;
   - the employer only has to do what is reasonably practicable to achieve this end;
   - again employee should be entitled to back pay etc.;
   - continuity of employment is again protected.
7. Compensatory award:
   - broken down into two parts: a basic award, and a compensatory award;
   - the basic award is calculated in a similar way to that in redundancy – according to years' service x a week's pay or £270 (whichever is the lower);
   - so the current ceiling for the basic award is £8,100;
   - there is also a minimum for the basic award;
   - amount of compensatory award is what tribunal thinks is 'just and equitable in all the circumstances';
   - but it is subject to a complex method of calculation;
   - and in any case the statutory maximum for an unfair dismissal award is currently £55,000;
   - except that there is no statutory limit for discrimination claims – since *Marshall (No.2)* and high awards have been granted (*MOD v Hunt* (1996)), (*MOD v Cannock* (1995));
   - and under s32 Employment Relations Act 1999 there is also now no statutory limit for a dismissal connected to asserting any HASAW right;
   - and by ERA 1999 s37 there is no upper limit for a dismissal for 'whistle blowing' under the Public Interest Disclosure Act 1998;
   - but otherwise ERA will not allow recovery for non-economic loss in unfair dismissal (*Dunnachie v Kingston-upon-Hull City Council* (2004)).

8. Following the Employment Rights (Dispute Resolution) Act 1998 an ACAS Arbitration Scheme was introduced on May 1st 2001 – it can be used provided that:
- the claim is solely for unfair dismissal;
- the claim contains no jurisdictional issues e.g. disputes over whether there was a dismissal or whether the employee had sufficient service;
- there are no complex legal issues to determine;
- both parties wish to use arbitration.

9. Under the procedure both parties then sign an arbitration agreement:
- and the claim can no longer be heard in a tribunal;
- the arbitrator does not apply strict legal tests or past case law, and there is no set format;
- any decision is reached by taking into account ACAS handbooks and good practice.

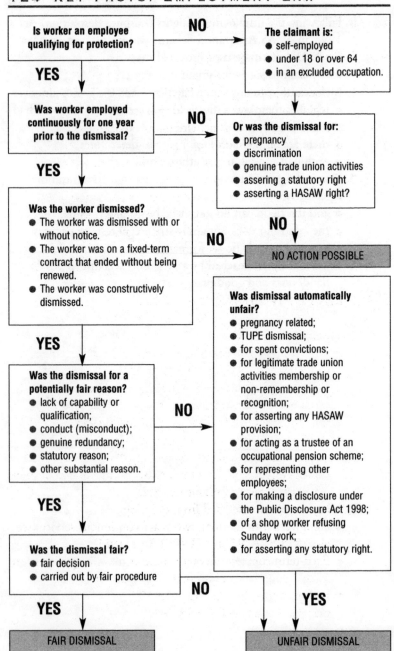

Diagram showing process for deciding if dismissal is fair or unfair

9.4 REDUNDANCY

9.4.1 General background

1. Introduced in Redundancy Payments Act 1965 with aims:
- highlight employees' needs for job security;
- make employer consider alternatives to dismissal;
- provide compensation for loss of work;
- encourage mobility and rationalisation of resources.

2. Compensation is:
- based on an uncomplicated system of calculation;
- paid for loss suffered, not as tide-over payment;
- payable even though employee finds other work;
- not taxable or a disqualification from claiming benefit.

3. In Part XI ERA 1996, and for collective TULR[C]A 1992.

9.4.2 Eligibility for redundancy

1. Three initial requirements:
- there must be a dismissal – either:
  - (i)   a dismissal with or without notice; or
  - (ii) a legitimate claim of constructive dismissal; or
  - (iii) a person accepted as a volunteer.
- the dismissal must be for reasons of redundancy;
- the person to be made redundant must be:
  - (i)   an employee (subject to usual tests); or
  - (ii) an employee under a fixed-term contract of two or more years, expiring without renewal.

2. Many people are excluded from claiming:
- employees with less than two years' continuous service (see also s218 ERA '96 and TU(PE) Regs. 1981);
- fixed-term contract of two or more years with agreement to forego redundancy rights – s197(3) ERA '96;
- persons under 20 – s211(2) ERA '96;
- persons over 65 – s156 ERA '96;
- share fishermen;

Eligibility

Three requirements:

- Dismissal:
  - with or without notice; or
  - legitimate constructive dismissal; or
  - person accepted as volunteer.
- For reasons of redundancy;
- Employee under fixed-term of over two years expiring without renewal.

People excluded from redundancy:

- under two years' continuous service;
- fixed-term contract of two or more years and waived redundancy rights;
- persons under 20;
- persons over 65;
- share fishermen;
- domestic servants of relatives;
- usually employed outside GB;
- employees of foreign governments;
- civil servants, some public officials;
- approved collective agreements;
- strikers, people dismissed for misconduct, and those refusing offers of suitable alternative employment.

Dismissal for reasons of redundancy

Statutory presumption unless contrary proved (*Tipper v Roofdec*).

- So employer has burden to show other reason (*Sanders v Ernest Neale*).

Redundancy only occurs if:

- employer ceases business;
- business ceases at employee's place of work;
- work diminishes.

Cessation straightforward – but can include temporary (*Gemmell v Darngavil Brickworks Ltd*).

Cessation at employee's place of work may be subject to mobility clause (*Bass Leisure Ltd v Thomas*).

Diminution follows re-organisation or change in work patterns e.g.:

- decline in work (*Hindle v Percival Boats*);
- change in character of work (*Murphy v Epsom College*);
- dramatic changes in condition (*MacFisheries v Findlay*).

But not mere changes in time of work (*Johnson v Nottinghamshire Combined Police Authority*). Whether there is a diminution is measured factually (*Murray v Foyle Meats Ltd*).

REDUNDANCY

Calculating payment

½ week pay per year's service – 18–21
1 week pay per " " – 22–40
1½ week's pay per " " – 41–64
up to max 20 years and 270 per week.

Procedure

- Must be based on sufficient warning, meaningful consultation, objective criteria for selection, selection criteria used (*Williams v Compare Maxim*).
- Should consider alternative strategies (*Allwood v William Hill*).
- Suitable alternative employment, if offered, should be on terms no less favourable to the job lost (*Taylor v Kent CC*).
- proper consultation procedure in s188 TULR[C]A 1992 – includes set time scale, requirement for genuine consultation, disclosure to unions of reasons for redundancy, numbers involved, criteria for selection, method of calculating pay if different to statutory minimum.
- Mass redundancies of 100 in 90 days or 20 in 30 days require notifying Secretary of State.
- Certain redundancies will be automatically unfair – if other workers in similar positions not selected e.g. pregnant workers, protected shopworkers etc.

- domestic servants of close relatives – s161 ERA '96;
- usually employed outside GB – s196(6) ERA '96;
- employees of foreign governments – s160 ERA '96;
- civil servants and certain public officials – s159 ERA '96;
- under approved collective agreements s157 ERA '96;
- strikers, people dismissed for misconduct, and those refusing offers of suitable alternative employment.

9.4.3 Dismissals for reasons of redundancy

1. Statutory presumption of redundancy unless contrary proved – s163(2) (*Vaux & Associated Breweries v Ward* and *Tipper v Roofdec* (1968)):
   - but employer can challenge presumption (*Chapman v Goonvean & Rostowrack China Clay Co.* (1973));
   - though employer has burden of proof to show other reason (*Sanders v Ernest Neale* (1974));
   - if none shown then presumption applies;
   - even if reason shown it may still be unfair dismissal.
2. By s139 ERA redundancy only occurs in three situations:
   - cessation of business for which employee employed;
   - cessation of business at employee's place of work;
   - diminution of work employee does under contract.
3. Cessation usually considered straightforward:
   - and temporary cessation may still cause redundancy (*Gemmell v Darngavil Brickworks Ltd* (1967));
   - problems can arise in defining business (*Thomas v Jones* (1978)).
4. Cessation at place of work may mean transfer rather than dismissal and there may be an express mobility clause:
   - if not, Tribunal may consider if implied term exists, compare *O'Brien v Associated Fire Alarms Co.* (1969) and *Managers (Holborn) Ltd v Hohne* (1977) and *Stevenson v Teesside Bridge & Engineering Ltd* (1971);
   - geographical test preferred to construction of contract recently (*Bass Leisure Ltd v Thomas* (1994));
   - but depends whether suitable alternative employment.

5. Diminution can lead to claims of unfair selection:
   - it can follow reduced demand, or re-organisation, change in work patterns;
   - may involve a decline in the work to be done by the employee (*Hindle v Percival Boats* (1969));
   - or total change in the character of work done (*Murphy v Epsom College* (1985));
   - or diminished need for specialist skills but need for new skills instead (*BBC v Farnworth* (1998));
   - but not a mere failure to adapt to new working methods (*North Riding Garages v Butterwick* (1967));
   - while dramatic changes in conditions might constitute a redundancy (*MacFisheries v Findlay* (1985));
   - changes in the time of work do not always amount to a redundancy (*Johnson v Nottinghamshire Combined Police Authority* (1974) and *Lesney Products Ltd v Nolan* (1977)).

6. Tribunals have also been called to decide whether definition of redundancy is 'factual' or 'contractual':
   - issue arises on question of what is 'place where the employee is employed' (*High Table v Horst* (1997)) – test was said to be 'consideration of factual circumstances and common sense of Tribunal';
   - and on diminution of 'work of a particular kind' (*Church v West Lancashire NHS Trust* (1998)) – here that test was rejected – test instead was that work in question should be that actually done by the employee – may be restrictive on employer trying to retain most able employees;
   - now apparently settled by HL in *Murray v Foyle Meats Ltd (Northern Ireland)* (1999), simple question is purely factual: has there been a diminution of the type of work required from the worker and was the dismissal solely attributable to this state of affairs?

9.4.4 Procedure on making redundancies

1. In *Williams v Compare Maxim* (1982) EAT laid out guidelines (not law) for good practice in redundancies:

- sufficient warning for parties to consider alternatives;
- proper and meaningful consultation with unions;
- objective criteria for selection, with no bias;
- selection accurately reflecting criteria set;
- identify reasonable alternative employment if possible.

2. So fair redundancy based on employer observing all these or may lead to successful unfair dismissal claim.

3. Consideration of alternatives to redundancy:
   - reasonable employer will consider possible alternatives first;
   - may include restricting recruitment, retraining, cutting overtime, job-sharing (*Allwood v William Hill* (1974));
   - or taking reasonable steps to absorb employees elsewhere – suitable alternative employment;
   - if employer offers suitable alternative employment on termination or within four weeks, and employee refuses, then loses right to redundancy pay – s138 ERA;
   - must be on terms no less favourable – and should take pay, status, hours, conditions etc. into account (*Taylor v Kent County Council* (1969));
   - refusal to accept must be reasonable or redundancy pay lost (*Fuller v Stephanie Bowman Ltd* (1977)).

4. Proper Consultation Procedure:
   - failure to properly consult or warn may lead to unfair dismissal claim (*Heron v Citylink Nottingham* (1993));
   - merely indicating redundancy or selection criteria will not (*Polkey v A.E. Dayton Services Ltd* (1983));
   - consultation required whenever employer 'proposing' to make more than 20 employees redundant – one issue being whether consultation is required when the proposal is conditional on other factors (*Scotch Premier Meat Ltd v Burns* (2000));
   - what counts as a redundancy for the purpose of consultation is wider than for other rights (*GMB v Man Truck & Bus UK Ltd* (2000)).

5. Procedure for collective redundancies in ss188–192 TULR[C]A '92 amended by Transfer of Undertakings (Protection of Employment) (Amendment) Regulations 1995

(to comply with Directive 75/129):

- union and other representatives must have proper access to redundant workers;
- time scale if dismissal within 90 days is: 90 days before relevant date if 100 employees or more, 30 days if between 20 and 100 employees;
- consultation must be genuine;
- so employer must disclose:
  (i) reasons for redundancy;
  (ii) number and descriptions of redundancies;
  (iii) total number of workers fitting description;
  (iv) proposed method of selection;
  (v) proposed method of dismissals;
  (vi) proposed method of calculating pay if different to statutory scheme.
- Secretary of State must be informed if 100 plus to go in 90 days or 20 plus in 30 – s193 TULR[C]A '92.

6. Proper Selection Procedure:

- tribunal may examine selection for fairness;
- unfair selection is unfair dismissal;
- originally LIFO (last in first out) but not appropriate or practical now;
- pre-arranged procedure must be followed;
- may use other criteria (*Selby v Plessey* (1972));
- criteria only has to be fair in general terms (*Clyde Pipeworks v Foster* (1978));
- ultimate test is not who tribunal would have selected but did employer act reasonably within the criteria;
- discriminatory criteria is also unfair dismissal (*Clarke v Eley (IMI) Kynoch Ltd* (1983));
- selecting the following is automatically unfair if other employees holding similar jobs are not selected:
  (i) pregnant workers – s94; those on parental or dependant care leave;
  (ii) on HASAW activities – s100;
  (iii) protected shopworkers refusing to work Sundays – s101;
  (iv) trustees of occupational pension s102;

(v)   employee reps under TULR[C]A '92;
(vi) workers exercising a statutory right – s104; or under
       Working Time regulations, Part-time regulations, Fixed
       term contract regulations, Minimum Wage Act etc;
(vii) union membership, non-membership, or activities –
       TULR[C]A '92 ss 152–153.

9.4.5 Calculating redundancy payments

1. Limitation period for making claim to ET is six months.
2. Entitlement is based on continuous service.
3. Payment is based on 'a normal week's wage'.
4. Scale is:

$^1/_2$ week's pay for each full year of service from 18–21
1   "   "   "   "   "   "   "   "   "   22–40
$1^1/_2$ "   "   "   "   "   "   "   "   "   41–64

subject to a maximum of 20 years, and a maximum of
£270 per week (figure requires regular updating under s34
Employment Relations Act 1999).

5. If employer insolvent employee may make claim for payment
from Secretary of State (*Smith v Secretary of State for Trade and
Industry* (1999)).

9.4.6 Lay offs and Short time

1. A lay off is any week in which an employee is available for
work but (s)he receives no pay.
2. Short time is a week in which employee receives under half pay.
3. If either carries on for four consecutive weeks or for six weeks
out of a 13 week period then the employee can claim to be
redundant.
4. An employee must serve notice to that effect to employer.
5. Employer may make successful counterclaim that proof exists
of a reasonable prospect of normal working patterns returning.

10.1 COURTS AND TRIBUNALS HEARING EMPLOYMENT CASES

European Court of Justice
- References for a preliminary ruling under A234 (formerly A177) on interpretation of a matter of EC law subject to the criteria set in the *CILFIT* case – that they are necessary to determine the issue.
- In UK they may be made by any court or tribunal – but must be made if the forum is the final hearing of the case.

House of Lords
- In practice few cases would be heard here – because they must involve a point of law of public importance.

Court of Appeal (Civil Division)
- The usual venue for appeals from the EAT.

The Employment Appeals Tribunal
- Actually a procedure in the High Court rather than a tribunal.
- Employment is unusual as an area where disputes are settled in tribunals in having its own specific appeal system.

County Court
- Certain cases can still be dealt with as traditional common law breach of contract actions.

Employment Tribunal
- Cases can be brought by an individual, by his/her union or even by one of the protective bodies such as EOC or CRE.

Time limits and originating procedure

All claims within three months except:

- for redundancy payments, dismissal after industrial action, unlawful expulsion from TU, equal pay – all six months;
- basic period can be extended where not possible to submit earlier.

Applicant submits claim form with details of:

- complaint, personal details, any representation, employer, employment, remedy sought.

Regional Office sends with notice of appearance to respondent – to be returned within 23 days.
Completed forms sent to ACAS. If no resolution then Tribunal date set.

Conciliation, Preliminary Hearings, Discovery and Inspection

Conciliation:

- ACAS has statutory duty to reach voluntary settlement – in confidential conciliation.
- 70% settle with compensation.
- Settlement recorded on COT3, no hearing.

Preliminary Review:

- Derives from Industrial Tribunal (Constitution and Rules of Procedure) Regulations 1993.
- Either party can seek one or Tribunal can suggest one.
- Happens because one party's case is weak.
- Any interested party can attend.
- Review inspects documents and suggests withdrawing case, if no prospect of success.
- £500 deposit to continue after this.

Disclosure and Inspection:

- May request to further and better particulars or disclosure of relevant documents.
- Tribunal can order where party's case is otherwise prejudiced.
- Striking out powers for non-compliance.
- Public Interest Privilege can apply.

Hearings

Hearings are public.
Composition:

- legally qualified chair;
- employer organisation representative;
- TU representative.

Inquisitorial, no rules of evidence.
Burden of proof shifts with type of claim.
Tribunal can reach decision in absence of party and strike out for misbehaviour – and general striking out power now possible.
Must give effect to the law as laid out by Parliament.
Oral decision given followed by reasoned decision later.
Costs limit now £10,000.

TRIBUNAL PROCEDURE

Remedies

Three basic ones:

- Reinstatement – returning to same job – no loss of rights.
- Re-engagement – return to different job – no worse conditions.
- Compensation – basic award (as for redundancy) _ compensatory award – ceiling £55,000 – but none in discrimination.

Recent developments

Following Employment Tribunal (Constitution and Procedure) Regulations 2001:

- Overriding objective to deal with cases justly.
- New case management powers similar to CPR.
- Weak cases deterred by increase in deposits and costs.
- In striking out word 'frivolous' replaced by misconceived.
- Must bear in mind Human Rights Act.

10.2 TRIBUNAL PROCEDURE

10.2.1 Time limits

1. Time limits govern employment tribunal procedure as with any other form of dispute resolution.
2. Interim relief applications – within seven days of dismissal.
3. All claims must be within three months of event except:
   - claim for redundancy payment must be within six months of termination (by s164 ERA 1996 tribunal can extend where just and equitable);
   - claim for dismissals after official industrial action must be within six months;
   - claims concerning unlawful exclusion or expulsion from trade unions also require six months;
   - equal pay claims must be presented within six months.
4. Tribunal can extend basic period where shown not to have been reasonably practicable to submit earlier – extension is for period tribunal considers reasonable in circumstances.
5. Rules for posting claims: first class mail – claim expected second working day after posting; second class mail – claim expected fourth working day after posting.

10.2.2 Originating procedure

1. Claimant fills in claim form (currently IT1 but new form from April 2005) including following details:
   - nature and details of complaint e.g. unfair dismissal;
   - personal details;
   - details of representation – if appropriate;
   - employer's details;
   - details of employment – including job description, length of service, pay, hours;
   - remedy sought;
   - confirmation that employee has raised issue with employer 28 days before to conform with SDDP.

2. Sends completed claim to local Regional Tribunal Office.
3. Regional Office then responds in following ways:
   - case number allotted and claim checked
   - applicant sent acknowledgement of receipt of claim;
   - respondent sent claim form and response form (on which to answer applicant's claim in detail).
4. Respondent returns completed IT3 to Regional Office within 23 days:
   - if 23 day time limit impossible then must be returned at earliest possible moment with explanatory note;
   - if respondent fails to return completed form then loses right to take part in proceedings (may still be called as witness or reach settlement with applicant).
5. On receipt Regional Office send forms to ACAS.
6. If ACAS unsuccessful then tribunal hearing date set:
   - parties must get minimum 14 days notice of hearing;
   - hearing date can be changed for good reason if Office notified;
   - parties may file further points any time up to seven days before hearing date – tribunal has wide powers to allow amendments to claim if justice served;
   - tribunal can be cancelled if parties reach mutually agreeable settlement – over half of claims are settled without hearing, many after conciliation proceedings.

10.2.3 Conciliation

1. ACAS has statutory duty to assist parties to reach a voluntary settlement.
2. Does so through process of conciliation hearings – whether in person, or by phone, individually, or together.
3. Communications are confidential and cannot be revealed to tribunal without that party's consent.
4. 70% of cases referred to conciliation are settled.
5. Where a voluntary agreement is reached this is recorded and filed and the tribunal is abandoned.

10.2.4 Pre-hearing review

1. Regulations provide for a pre-hearing review.
2. Either party can apply for such a review or the tribunal might demand it.
3. Occurs because a party's case is weak or unsustainable.
4. Any relevant parties may attend review (e.g. party's representative) which is usually conducted before chairman.
5. Either party may submit written representations in advance.
6. Review inspects documentation so far submitted (i.e. IT1 and IT3).
7. If claim considered to have no prospect of success then chairman tells party concerned who is expected to withdraw (not obliged to – but may be penalised if continues and case is lost).
8. If party wishes to continue then must pay deposit of £500.

10.2.5 Discovery and inspection

1. A party may request further and better particulars or discovery (now called disclosure) of relevant documents.
2. Since tribunals take non-legalistic approach there is no automatic procedure for discovery and inspection of documents – tribunal can make such orders at request of a party, if it is shown case is prejudiced without them.
3. If order not complied with then tribunal may strike out whole or part of defence or claim to which it relates.
4. Rules on privilege from disclosure apply if in public interest.

10.2.6 Hearings

1. Hearings are public so press can attend and report.
2. They can be heard in private on application of one party – if there is substantial cause.
3. Restricted reporting in cases alleging sexual misconduct.
4. Composition of a tribunal is as follows:
   - legally qualified member – usually the chair;
   - member drawn from panel approved by Secretary of State representing employers' organisations;

- member drawn from panel approved by Secretary of State representing trade union/employee association.
5. Order of proceedings resemble court – but rules of evidence do not apply and forum is inquisitorial as members of panel may take active part in questioning.
6. Burden of proof varies with issue e.g. if unfair dismissal alleged under a potentially fair head then employer must show it was fair.
7. Party with burden opens – makes opening statement, calls witnesses and introduces all other evidence:
   - other party then repeats the same process together with closing speech;
   - either party may cross examine witnesses, and re-examination is possible as in a normal trial;
   - first party gives a closing speech;
   - tribunal deliberates and gives its decision.
8. Tribunal can reach a decision in absence of either party – after due consideration of any written representation – and may dismiss application if applicant fails to attend.
9. Tribunal may strike out proceedings for misbehaviour of a party – Secretary of State for Trade and Industry has now introduced a general striking out power for tribunals.
10. Tribunal's duty in reaching a decision is to give effect to the law as laid down by Parliament – although they may interpret ambiguous words in a provision.
11. About 95% of tribunal decisions are unanimous.
12. Oral decisions are usually given in tribunal – but also bound to deliver a reasoned decision, done at later date.
13. Costs limit is £10,000.
14. Procedure now governed by Employment Tribunals (Constitution and Rules of Procedure) Regulations 2004.

10.2.7 New developments in procedure

1. Employment Tribunal (Constitution and Procedure) Regulations 2004 includes provisions to speed up process and discourage weak claims.

2. Overriding objective is similar to that in the CPR – so tribunal can deal with cases 'justly' – it should as far as practicable:
   - ensure parties are on equal footing;
   - save expense;
   - deal with cases in way proportionate to their degree of complexity;
   - ensure cases are dealt with expeditiously and fairly.
3. Schedule 1 Rule 4 includes general case management powers:
   - Can 'give such directions on any matters arising in connection with proceedings as appear to the tribunal to be appropriate'.
   - Under Rule 4(3) this includes 'any requirements relating to evidence' (including the provision and exchange of witness statements), and the provision of further particulars.
4. Weak and hopeless cases can be deterred by the increase of the deposits from £150 to £500, and increase of costs orders from £500 to £10,000.
5. In relation to striking out the expression 'frivolous' is changed to 'misconceived' – misconceived is defined as 'having no reasonable prospect of success'.
6. There are also new rules in relation to cases involving national security.
7. The rules also stress need to bear in mind provisions of the Human Rights Act, in particular Article 6.

10.2.8 Remedies

1. Reinstatement: returning employee to same job as though dismissal never occurred – and compensation is available for the interim period.
2. Re-engagement: an order to re-employ employee, not in same position – but on substantially same conditions.
3. Compensation: includes basic award, and compensatory award (which in discrimination cases can include a sum for injured feelings):
   - basic award calculated as redundancy;

- current ceiling for unfair dismissal claims is £55,000;
- but no ceiling on discrimination claims;
- additional award available where employer fails to carry out order for reinstatement or re-engagement.

INDEX

absenteeism 118
ACAS
    conciliation 133, 135
    disciplinary codes 34
    discipline 33
    employment tribunals 135
    grievance procedures 32
    legal status 34
    tribunals 133
    unfair dismissal 123
adoption leave 50–1
agency workers 12
ante-natal care 45, 46
appeals, dismissal 120–1
arbitration
    see also ACAS
    unfair dismissal 123

blue pencilling 25, 29

care, duty of 41, 43
care leave, dependants 50–1
casual employment 11–12
collective agreements
    contracts of employment 20, 21,
        22–3
    definitions 20
    express incorporation 20–2
    implied incorporation 21, 22
    no-strike clauses 21, 23
    non-union employees 21, 22–3
    termination 21, 23
    transfer 104
    works rules 21, 23–4
compensation
    discrimination 78
    redundancy 126, 131
    unfair dismissal 115, 122–3

competitors, working for 27
conciliation see ACAS
confidentiality 39, 43
constructive dismissal 32, 107, 109
contracts of employment
    acceptance 14–15
    breaches 110
    collective agreements 20, 21, 22–3
    express terms 17, 18–20
    forms of 13, 14–15, 16
    illegal 13, 15
    implied terms 17, 18, 19
    job descriptions 24
    minors 13, 15
    s1 statements 16
    termination 109
    unfair 19
    variation 19
    wages 51
control test, employment 9, 10
County Courts 132
Court of Appeal 132

damages
    discrimination 84, 85
    wrongful dismissal 111, 112–13
defences
    contributory negligence 87
    health and safety 87, 92
dependants, care leave 50–1
directors 12
disabilities
    definitions 76
    dependants 50–1
    discrimination 75–8
    working conditions 77
disciplinary procedures
    and dismissals 38

hearings 33, 35–6
warnings 33, 37–8
discrimination
  see also racial discrimination; sex
    discrimination
  claims procedures 84–5
  compensation 78
  damages 84, 85
  definitions 67, 77
  direct 64, 65
  disabilities 75–8
  EU laws 83
  harassment 42, 67–8
  indirect 64, 65–6
  job advertisements 67
  lawful 64
  occupational 64
  positive 63
  pregnancy 69
  recruitment 66–7
  redundancy selection 68
  religious 83
  remedies 83, 85–6
  trade union membership 78–83
  unfair dismissal 68–9
  victimisation 64, 66
dismissals
  see also unfair dismissal; wrongful
    dismissal
  action short of 79, 80–1
  appeals 120–1
  constructive 32, 107, 109
  definitions 107, 109
  determining fairness 119–21
  and disciplinary procedures 38
  discriminatory 68–9, 72, 74
  health grounds 117–18
  implied terms 42
  industrial action 79, 82, 116
  justifications 116–18
  for misconduct 107, 109, 111, 118
  notice 29–30, 107, 108–9
  potentially fair 113, 116–19
  pregnancy 49–50, 114, 116
  procedures 109, 111
  reasonableness 120–1
  redundancy 118–19, 126–8
  summary 107, 109, 111
  trade union membership 79, 81–2,
    114–16
  transfer of undertakings 99,
    104–5, 115, 116
  tribunals 119–20
Donovan Commission 2

economic reality test, employment 9,
  11
employees
  capabilities 117
  competence 43
  confidentiality 43
  definitions 7–8, 7–9
  dishonesty 118
  enticement 27
  fidelity 43–4
  health and safety duties 90–1, 95
  health and safety of 116
  implied duties 39, 42–4
  mental health 90–1
  misconduct 107, 109, 111, 118
  notice 108–9
  qualifications 117–18
  references 91
  rights 2–4
  sickness 117–18
  skills 43
  transfer of undertakings 100–1,
    103–4
  working hours 98
employers
  disabled employees 77–8
  dismissal rights 116–19
  health and safety duties 87, 88–90,
    93–5
  implied duties 39, 41–2
employment
  casual 11–12
  continuity of 107, 108

definitions 9
refusal 64
rights 2
special forms of 11–12
tests of 9–11
Employment Appeals Tribunal 132
employment law, history 1–4
employment rights, trade unions
  78–9
Employment Tribunals 132, 135
  procedures 133, 134–8
  time limits 131
equal pay
  see also discrimination
  avoidance 58, 61–2
  comparitors 58, 59–60
  decision making 61
  equal value work 58, 59, 60–1
  equivalent work 58, 60
  EU laws 58, 59, 61–3
  genuine material factors 58
  'like work' 58, 59, 60
EU laws
  discrimination 83
  employment 3–6
  equal pay 58, 59, 61–3
  health and safety 92–3, 92–4, 96–7
  status 5–6
European Court of Justice 132
express incorporation, collective
  agreements 20–2
express terms
  advantages 17, 19
  contracts of employment 17,
    18–20
  disadvantages 17, 20
  interpreting 17, 19
  range of 17, 18

fidelity 39

garden leave 29–31
grievance procedures 42
  statutory 31–2

harassment, sexual 42, 67–8
health and safety
  common law origins 88
  contributory negligence 87, 88, 92
  defences 87, 92
  duties 87, 91
  employees' duties 90–1, 95
  employers' duties 87, 88–90, 93–5
  EU laws 92–3, 92–4, 96–7
  legislation 92–8
  mental health 90–1
  non-delegable duties 87, 89–90
  policy statements 93
  pregnancy 46–7, 50
  reasonableness 87, 91
  safe plant 89
  safe workplaces 89
  safety representatives 94
  staff competence 89
  unfair dismissal 116
  volenti 87, 91
  working time regulations 93–4
Health and Safety at Work Act
  (1974) 93–8
Health and Safety Commission 94,
  96
Health and Safety Executive 94, 96
Health and Safety Inspectorate 96
hearings, disciplinary 33, 35–6
hospital staff 12
House of Lords 132

implied duties
  employees 39, 42–4
  employers 39, 41–2
implied incorporation 21, 22
implied terms
  contracts of employment 17, 18,
    19
  dismissal 42
  employees' duties 39, 42–4
  employers' duties 39, 41–2
  incorporation 39, 40–1
Income Tax 8

Indicia Test, employment 10–11
industrial action, dismissal during 79, 82, 116
industrial disputes, pay during 57

job descriptions 24

lawful and reasonable instructions 42–3
lay-offs, pay 57
leave
    adoption 50–1
    care 50–1
    maternity 45, 47–8, 49
    parental 50–1

maternity
    see also pregnancy
    additional leave 45, 49
    allowances 48
    ante-natal care 45, 46
    discrimination 69
    leave 45, 47–8
    pay 45, 46, 48
    redundancy during 49
    return after 13, 14, 45, 49
    rights 46–9, 108
    suspension 46–7
    unfair dismissal 8, 49–50
mental health, employees 90–1
minimum wages 52, 56
minors, contracts of employment 13, 15
misconduct, dismissals for 107, 109, 111, 118
multiple test, employment 9, 11

National Insurance 8
National Minimum Wage Act (1998) 52, 56
NHS, transfers 101
no-strike clauses 21, 23
non-solicitation clauses 27

notice
    garden leave 29–31
    payments in lieu 55
    periods 55, 108–9
    statutory periods 107

occupational pensions 58, 62
Ordinary Person Test, employment 10
organisation test, employment 9, 10
outworkers 12

parental leave 50–1
part-time employees, rights 12
pay
    see also equal pay; wages
    deductions 52, 54–5
    definitions 58, 62
    guaranteed 57
    itemised statements of 53
    lay-offs 57
    maternity 45, 48
    minimum wages 52, 56
    notice periods 55, 108–9
    overpayment 52, 53, 55
    rights to 52
    short time 57
    sickness 52, 53–4
pensions
    discrimination 67
    occupational 58, 62
    sex discrimination 64
    transfer of undertakings 104, 106
pregnancy
    see also maternity
    discrimination 69
    health and safety 46–7, 50
    unfair dismissal 45, 49–50, 114–16
protection of interests
    client contacts 25, 26–7
    trade secrets 25
public interest 25
public sector, transfer of undertakings 101

quantum meruit, wages 51, 52

Race Relations Act (1965) 71–5
racial discrimination
  definitions 71–3
  direct 71–3
  employment 72, 73–4
  indirect 72, 73
  lawful 72, 75
  recruitment 74
  victimisation 72, 73
reasonable and lawful instructions 42
reasonableness
  care 39
  implied 39, 40, 42–3
  restraint on trade 25, 28
  skills 39
recruitment
  discrimination 66–7
  racial discrimination 74
redundancy
  alternative employment 126
  collective 129–30
  compensation 126, 131
  consultation 118–19, 126, 129
  definitions 128
  diminution 128
  discrimination 68
  dismissal 118–19, 126–8
  excluded persons 125–7
  lay-offs 131
  maternity leave 49
  procedures 119, 126, 129–31
  selection for 118–19, 128–9,
    130–1
  short term 131
  transfer of undertakings 127,
    129–30
  tribunals 128
  unfair 126, 130–1
references, duties to provide 91
reinstatement, unfair dismissal
  121–2

religious discrimination 83
restraint on trade
  definitions 25–6
  duration 28
  enforceability 26
  public interest 25
  reasonableness 25, 28
  void 28
Robens Committee (1970) 92–3
rule books 21, 23–4

safety *see* health and safety
safety representatives 94
self-employment 8
sex discrimination 63–71
  gays 70–1
  genuine occupational
    qualifications 64, 68–9
  lawful 68–9
  pensions 64
  transsexuals 64, 70–1
Sex Discrimination Act (1976)
  63–71
sexual harassment 42, 67–8
sexual orientation, discrimination 64
short time pay 57
sickness
  dismissal due to 117–18
  pay 52, 53–4
  periods of 52, 53–4
statutory rights, assertion of 116
sub-contractors 11
suspension, maternity 46–7

trade secrets 26
trade unions
  activities 79, 81
  collective agreements 20, 21,
    22–3
  discrimination 78–83
  dismissals for membership 79,
    81–2, 114–16
  employment rights 78–9, 79

industrial action 82
non-membership 21, 22–3
trainees, wages 55
transfer of undertakings
  application 99, 100–1
  consultations 99, 106
  definitions 101–3
  dismissals 99, 104–5, 115–16
  effects 99, 103–4
  nature of 99, 101–3
  pensions 104, 106
  redundancies 127, 129–30
transsexuals, discrimination 70–1
tribunals
  see also employment tribunals
  conciliation 133
  dismissal 119–20
  employment 132
  hearings 133, 136
  procedures 136–8
  redundancy 128
  remedies 133, 138–9
  time limits 133
trust, mutual 19, 42

unfair dismissal
  arbitration 123
  automatic 113, 115–16
  compensation 115, 122–3
  definition 111, 112
  determination of 124
  discrimination 68–9
  eligibility 114, 114–15, 115
  exclusions 114, 116
  health and safety 116
  industrial action 82, 115–16
  minimum pay assertions 55
  pregnancy 8, 45, 49–50, 114–16
  re-engagement 121, 122
  reasonableness 120–1
  reinstatement 121–2
  remedies 115, 124
  rights assertion 116

transfer of undertakings 105
tribunals 121–2

victimisation, sexual 64, 66
volenti, health and safety 87

wages
  see also pay
  contracts of employment 51
  definitions 55
  duty to pay 39, 41
  minimum 52, 56
  quantum meruit 51, 52
  rights to 39, 52, 53
  trainees 55
warnings, disciplinary 33, 37–8
work, right to 41
work rules 21, 23–4
working hours regulations 94, 98
working practices, safety 90
workplaces, safety 89
works rules 23–4
wrongful dismissal 111
  actions for 112
  damages 111, 112–13
  nature of 111

The law at your fingertips…with **Key Facts**

Series Editors: Jacqueline Martin and Chris Turner

Key Facts has been specifically written for students studying Law. It is the essential revision tool for a broad range of law courses from A Level to degree level.

The series is written and edited by an expert team of authors whose experience means they know exactly what is required in a revision aid. They include examiners, barristers and lecturers who have brought their expertise and knowledge to the series to make it user-friendly and accessible.

Key features:
- User-friendly layout and style
- Diagrams, charts and tables to illustrate key points
- Summary charts at basic level, followed by more detailed explanations, to aid revision at every level
- Pocket sized and easily portable
- Written by highly regarded authors and editors

The **Key Facts** series includes:

Consumer Law	0 340 88758 3	144pp	£5.99	NEW
Contract Law, 2nd ed.	0 340 88949 7	160pp	£5.99	NEW
Employment Law, 2nd ed.	0 340 88947 0	160pp	£5.99	NEW
Human Rights	0 340 88696 X	144pp	£5.99	NEW
Tort, 2nd edition	0 340 88948 9	160pp	£5.99	NEW
Company Law	0 340 84586 4	128pp	£5.99	
Constitutional & Administrative Law	0 340 81272 9	106pp	£5.99	
Criminal Law, 2nd ed.	0 340 88605 6	136pp	£5.99	
Equity & Trusts	0 340 87173 3	138pp	£5.99	
European Law	0 340 84584 8	136pp	£5.99	
Evidence	0 340 85935 0	152pp	£5.99	
Family Law	0 340 81474 8	168pp	£5.99	
Land Law, 2nd ed.	0 340 81563 9	112pp	£5.99	
The English Legal System	0 340 80179 4	120pp	£5.99	

Visit www.hoddereducation.co.uk for full details on how to order.

Unlocking the Law

Series Editors: Jacqueline Martin and Chris Turner

Unlocking the Law is a completely new series of textbooks with a unique approach to undergraduate study of law, designed specifically so that the subject matter is readable and that students are not overwhelmed with page after page of continuous prose.

The text of each title is broken up with features and activities that have been written to ensure that students are pointed in the right direction when it comes to understanding the purpose of different areas within the course. All titles in the series follow the same format and include the same features so that students can move easily from one law subject to another.

The series covers all the core subjects required by the Bar Council and the Law Society for entry onto professional qualifications and will expand to include titles on option areas.

Unlocking the Law includes the following titles:

Unlocking Constitutional & Administrative Law	0 340 81606 6	Publishing May 05
Unlocking Contract Law	0 340 81566 3	Available now
Unlocking Criminal Law	0 340 81565 5	Available now
Unlocking EU Law	0 340 88759 1	Publishing May 05
Unlocking Land Law	0 340 81564 7	Available now
Unlocking Legal Learning	0 340 88761 3	Publishing May 05
Unlocking The English Legal System	0 340 88693 5	Publishing May 05
Unlocking Torts	0 340 81567 1	Available now
Unlocking Trusts	0 340 88694 3	Publishing May 05

Visit www.unlockingthelaw.co.uk or www.hoddereducation.co.uk for full details on how to order.